IBM Cloud Platform Primer

Ashok K. Iyengar

MC Press Online, LLC
Boise, ID 83703 USA

IBM Cloud Platform Primer

Ashok K. Iyengar

First Edition

MC Press offers excellent discounts on this book when ordered in quantity for bulk purchases or special sales, which may include custom covers and content particular to your business, training goals, marketing focus, and branding interest.

MC Press Online, LLC

Corporate Offices: 3695 W. Quail Heights Court, Boise, ID 83703-3861 USA

Sales and Customer Service: (208) 629-7275 ext. 500;

service@mcpressonline.com

Permissions and Bulk/Special Orders: mcbooks@mcpressonline.com

www.mcpressonline.com • www.mc-store.com

ISBN: 978-1-58347-840-0   WB201509

Dedication

I dedicate this book to my mom, Jayalakshmi Iyengar, who at the age of 92 still spends most of her time reading. She has been through a lot in life, but nothing can dull her passion for reading. She reads books, magazines, newspapers, and even electronic media. Last Christmas, she was presented with a tablet by her grandson— a Kindle Fire HD—and now she, too, surfs the Internet for articles and news items and downloads books. What amazes me is not the technology per se, but that we've made technology simple enough that the young and the old can join us on our ride in the clouds.

About the Author

Ashok K. Iyengar is an executive IT specialist at IBM, based in San Diego. He holds a MS degree in computer science from North Dakota State University, Fargo, and has worked in the IT industry for over 30 years. In his spare time, he loves to write. Among Iyengar's works are the popular *WebSphere Business Integration Primer* (IBM Press, 2007) and *WebSphere Portal Primer* (IBM Press, 2005). For the past two years, he has worked on cloud-based projects doing proofs-of-concept, pilots, architecture design, and implementations.

Acknowledgments

This book would not have been possible without the help and understanding of a lot of people—family, friends, colleagues, and even strangers met while traveling. Above all, I am thankful to my wife, Radha, for her moral support and constant encouragement, and to our sons, Sameer and Siddharth, who continue to inspire me in ways I had not envisioned.

I owe a great deal of gratitude to my colleagues, Peter Van Sickel and Venkata "Vishy" Gadepalli, who not only were the driving force behind the technical content of the book but reviewed the material and provided invaluable feedback. I owe a very big "thank you" to Srinivas Chowdhury, Michele Chilanti, and Manav Gupta, who were always willing to review chapters and answer questions. Their collective expertise and feedback have gone a long way toward improving the content and flow of the book.

I tip my hat to my mentor, Kyle Brown, for his expert advice, vision, and direction.

I would be remiss to not thank Katie Tipton and the talented staff at MC Press, who have done an outstanding job of getting this book published. Thanks to Dan DiPinto for coming up with the cover design, to Barb Alexy for a marvelous job of copy editing, and to Anne Grubb for managing it all.

This page intentionally left blank.

Contents

This page intentionally left blank.

Foreword

There are about a million really bad cloud metaphors. I could tell you how this book helps you "see through the haze" surrounding cloud computing. I could also tell you how it "lifts the fog" from understanding IaaS, PaaS, and all the other cloud acronyms. Finally, I could tell you how it can make your life sunnier by showing you how IBM's cloud computing products can help you become better at deploying and managing software in both private and public clouds. But I wouldn't dare insult your intelligence by starting with any of those overwrought comparisons.

Instead, how about I state simply what you'll gain from reading this book. You'll gain an understanding of IBM's unique approach to cloud computing. IBM's approach differs from that of many of what you may consider the "born-on-the-cloud" companies, such as Amazon and Google, in that it first considers the special needs and concerns of enterprise developers. For instance, it may be well and good if you write an athletic event application using Node.js and a NoSQL database that may not always show registrations at the very second that they are submitted due to queries done on other nodes and the ramifications of the CAP theorem. However, inconsistency of that sort would be absolutely fatal in a core banking application. Likewise, the development and DevOps approaches that work for a team that can all share a single pizza will not necessarily work in a globally distributed, hundred-developer team that is building critical policy-management software for a heavily regulated health insurer.

What Ashok and his team of technical editors have managed to do successfully is to explain how IBM's unique viewpoint—one that adopts cloud terminology and open cloud technologies while remaining cognizant of its enterprise development heritage—has influenced the development of our cloud products. You'll see how we introduced the notion of patterns of expertise to help enterprise developers migrate their large-scale applications built on enterprise-ready middleware into cloud computing approaches. You'll see how IBM Bluemix provides a PaaS built on open standards that still addresses the needs of the enterprise—for security, for scalability and reliability, and for access to on-premises enterprise IT systems. You'll understand how to use new container approaches, such as Docker. And you'll also gain an understanding of how offerings such as SoftLayer help you make the best choice for your cloud; be it a public, private, or semi-private cloud in either a virtualized or bare-metal model.

The key is deciding what's right for your particular requirements and not being locked into a single model that a vendor has decided is right for every case. IBM's approach is more that you need freedom to choose from different options, rather than being forced into a one-size-fits-all approach.

So turn the page, sit back, and enjoy the ride. I certainly did, and I'm sure you will too.

Kyle Brown
IBM Distinguished Engineer

1

The Cloud at Your Service

C loud computing is a way to use and share hardware, operating systems, storage, and network capacity over the Internet. Cloud service providers rent virtualized servers, storage, and networking components to consumers to use on demand, as needed. The advantages are many. Cloud service providers can constantly update services and hardware, upgrade features, and add new ones, so consumers can stay on top of the technology wave without investing directly in infrastructure and, in some cases, applications. That frees companies to focus on their specific businesses and avoid much of the cost of purchasing, maintaining, upgrading, and troubleshooting hardware and software. In the cloud provisioning model, consumers subscribe to services on a pay-as-you-go basis or over a fixed period of time, most commonly by the month or year, and they pay only for what they use. Consumers also have the option of hosting their own cloud environment for security and compliance reasons.

Although the underlying concepts of cloud computing are not new, with the advent of new tools and technologies, these concepts have matured, and the cloud now can provide services efficiently, securely, and at a massive scale. From a hardware perspective, there is Infrastructure as a Service (IaaS). From a software angle, we have applications or Software as a Service (SaaS). And for blended offerings, there is Platform as a Service (PaaS). The benefit of all these approaches is that they reduce the enterprise's total cost of owning and maintaining computing resources.

This chapter discusses cloud computing in general and presents a reference architecture for cloud computing. The concepts of virtualization and workload deployment are common to all platforms from any vendor.

Cloud Computing

This book follows the National Institute of Standards and Technology (NIST) definition of cloud computing: "Cloud computing is a model for enabling convenient, on-demand network access to a shared pool of configurable computing resources (e.g., networks, servers, storage, applications, and services) that can be rapidly provisioned and released with minimal management effort or service provider interaction." There are five widely recognized essential characteristics of cloud computing.

- Broad network access—First and foremost, all cloud-related services must be available and accessible ubiquitously over the network via standard mechanisms that promote use by heterogeneous thick or thin clients. Clients can range from workstations and laptops to tablets and smart devices.

- On-demand self-service—Consumers must be able to unilaterally and automatically provision services as needed, without requiring human interaction. The services can range from simple email applications to applications that require server time and network storage. On-demand services are exemplified by Google's Gmail and Amazon's Amazon Web Services (AWS).

- Resource pooling—The provider's computing resources, such as memory, processing, storage, network bandwidth, and even virtual machines (VMs), must be pooled to serve multiple consumers using a multi-tenant model. The multi-tenant model dynamically assigns and reassigns location-transparent physical and virtual resources based on consumer demand.

- Rapid elasticity—The basic difference between traditional computing and cloud computing is the provisioning capability. In cloud computing, resources and services must be able to rapidly and automatically scale up when needed and be released or scaled down when they are not. To the consumer, these services and resources usually appear to be unlimited and can be appropriated in any quantity at any time.

- Metering of services—Because cloud computing employs a pay-per-use model, resource usage must be able to be measured, controlled, and reported transparently to both the provider and consumer of the service. Thus, cloud systems must have a metering capability that can control and optimize resource use.

In addition to these five essentials, the Cloud Security Alliance (*www.cloud securityalliance.org*) advocates a sixth characteristic of cloud computing:

- Multi-tenancy—Implicit in the way cloud computing hosts tenants is a need for policy-driven enforcement, segmentation, isolation, governance, service levels, and chargeback/billing models for different consumer constituencies. Multi-tenancy comes into play when consumers utilize a provider's public cloud service offerings.

These six characteristics lend themselves to certain service delivery models, the main ones being IaaS, PaaS, and SaaS. Figure 1.1 shows the relationship between these and other cloud service layers. A provider can choose to offer one or more of these services.

IaaS

IaaS deals primarily with hosting the environment. Infrastructure as a Service is the new way to use and share hardware, operating systems, storage, and network capacity over the Internet. Instead of using slices and logical partitioning, consumers can

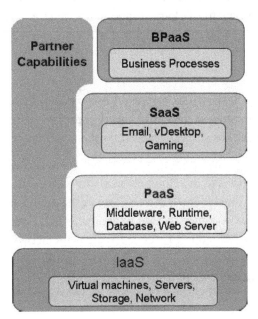

Figure 1.1: Cloud service layers

now rent virtualized servers, storage, and networking components. The consumer can provision processing, storage, networks, and other fundamental computing resources, then deploy and run arbitrary software, which can include operating systems and applications. The consumer does not manage or control the underlying cloud infrastructure, but does have control over the operating system, storage, and deployed applications, and possibly limited control of select networking components, such as switches in the datacenter and ports.

As in the old mainframe days, the service provider owns the equipment and is responsible for housing it, running it, and maintaining it. The characteristics of today's IaaS are

- self service via the Internet

- dynamic scaling, sometimes referred to as elasticity

- policy-based services

- utility computing billing

In the IaaS provisioning model, the consumer pays for the infrastructure on a per-use basis. A major benefit of cloud computing in general and IaaS in particular is that it allows companies to avoid up-front infrastructure costs and focus on business-related projects.

PaaS

As we move up the stack shown in Figure 1.1, we come to the computing platform, which includes the operating system, an execution engine, database, and Web server. Cloud vendors package these services and offer them as Platform as a Service.

PaaS concentrates on the building and deployment aspect of the cloud. Consumers can deploy applications to the cloud infrastructure using programming languages, libraries, services, and tools that the provider supports. Applications are typically middleware and can be consumer-created or acquired. The consumer does not manage or control the underlying cloud infrastructure such as the network, servers, or storage, but does have control over the deployed applications and possibly over configuration settings for the hosting environment.

PaaS resources can be used to run existing applications or develop and test new ones. Application developers have to worry only about developing their apps and running them on the platform as and when needed. Some vendors offer automatic scaling of computing and storage resources to match application demand.

 Note: New applications created on cloud platforms are termed "born on the cloud."

Vendors of PaaS cloud services not only provide the infrastructure but also manage it and support client applications. Vendors can continually update services and add new features. PaaS providers can assist developers from the conception of original ideas to creating, testing, and deploying applications.

Vendors typically include the following resources and features in a PaaS offering:

- operating system
- database
- middleware
- server-side scripting
- compute nodes
- storage
- network access
- development and test tools
- maintenance and support

PaaS has several advantages for software developers because operating system complexities are hidden, while the resources and features are easily accessible and can be increased or decreased according to demand. Development teams may be geographically distributed, yet are still able to work together on software projects. Services can be obtained from diverse sources, some of which may be on-premises while others are hosted on remote systems across the globe. Enterprises can reduce setup and ongoing costs and eliminate unnecessary duplication of functions by using infrastructure services from a single vendor rather than maintaining multiple hardware facilities on their own. And IT expenses can be minimized by sharing services and repositories and centralizing software development and test environments.

It's important to mention the subtle differences between PaaS and traditional distributed systems. Tasks such as continuous integration, build, deploy, and test are automated and repeatable. PaaS resources can be scaled up or conserved according to policies and need, and platform-neutral scripting makes it possible for applications to interact with the system firmware. In short, PaaS lets systems administrators focus on systems rather than servers, helps architects evaluate new technology quickly and directly, and enables IT developers to quickly develop and test projects.

On the downside, there are some pitfalls to be aware of. PaaS involves some risk of "lock-in" if offerings require proprietary service interfaces or development languages. And the flexibility of offerings might not meet the needs of users whose requirements evolve rapidly.

SaaS

Software as a Service is all about consumption. SaaS hosts software and applications on the cloud and delivers them to consumers as a service, sometimes referred to as "on-demand software." The consumer uses the provider's applications, which run on a cloud infrastructure. Although the applications are ubiquitously accessible, the consumer does not manage or control the underlying cloud infrastructure—not even the individual applications. The only aspects that the consumer has some control over are who can access the software and user-specific application configuration settings.

In most cases, users access SaaS via a thin client, such as a Web browser. SaaS is a common delivery model for everything from simple word processing software to enterprise resource planning, business process management, and customer relationship management software. Customer relationship management is the largest market for SaaS, but this delivery model is also used for business applications such as messaging, database management, and business management applications.

One of the main selling points of SaaS is the potential to reduce IT costs by outsourcing hardware and software maintenance and support to the SaaS provider. The pricing model for SaaS applications is typically a monthly or yearly flat fee per user, so the cost of the service is predictable and adjusted whenever users are added or removed.

Another cloud service layer that is garnering attention is Business Process as a Service, or BPaaS. A type of business process outsourcing, BPaaS is any horizontal or vertical business process—transaction processing, for example—that is delivered via the cloud services model. BPaaS minimizes up-front capital expenditures and reduces operational expenses. Some argue that BPaaS is simply a specialized SaaS offering similar to desktop as a service, communication as a service, or database as a service (DBaaS). A good debate is a learning experience.

Responsibilities

Figure 1.2 is a different way of looking at what constitutes cloud services and specifically at who is responsible for the various components. In the traditional IT department, the organization buys all hardware and software, houses it in a data center, and is in charge of running the operations. In cloud jargon, this approach is known as on-premises systems, and the client either manages the resources in-house or outsources management to an IT operations company.

Notice that as you move from left (IaaS) to right (SaaS), responsibility shifts from the client to the cloud provider. Divesting operations that are not directly related to the business is a benefit to the client. A retail company can concentrate on making

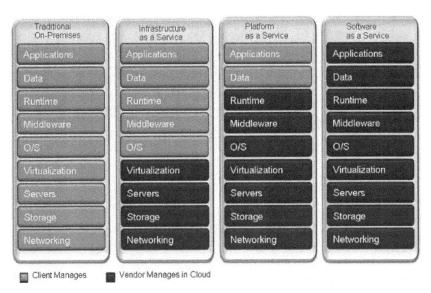

Figure 1.2: Separation of responsibilities

and marketing its products and not have to worry about managing its computing hardware or software, for example. In addition, by letting a cloud vendor manage things, the client is assured of getting and working with the latest in technology.

Although cloud computing proponents point to the cost savings and agility of such an environment, some IT organizations view it as a threat to their roles and a challenge to their expertise. Chapter 8 discusses how the cloud is changing IT roles and responsibilities.

Cloud Computing Reference Architecture

Reference architectures serve as a blueprint for architects and practitioners in the design of a solution or a "to-be" model. A Cloud Computing Reference Architecture (CCRA) assists in the design of public and private clouds. Specifically, it helps developers define scope and make architectural decisions, thus assisting teams in delivering consistent design and project results. Most reference architectures are created over time, based on experiences and real-world implementations.

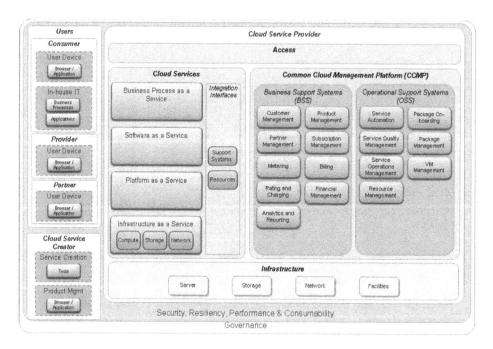

Figure 1.3: IBM's CCRA

At a high level, the major actors of a CCRA are a cloud service creator, a cloud service provider, and a cloud service consumer. The reference architecture may also include a cloud broker and cloud auditor. Figure 1.3 shows a pictorial representation of a CCRA that's based on the IBM® CCRA.

Although the cloud service provider seems to occupy the largest chunk of territory in Figure 1.3, service creators play a big role, and service consumers are also key actors. The ease with which consumers can access and use services is the hallmark of a successful implementation of the CCRA.

Cloud-Ready vs. Cloud-Centric Applications

The terms *cloud-ready* and *cloud-centric* describe the constitution of applications meant for the cloud. The distinction between these two terms is straightforward. When an existing application is deployed into either a private or public cloud, it is known as a cloud-ready or migrated-to-the-cloud application. New applications that are created specifically to run on the cloud are known as cloud-centric or born-on-the-cloud.

This distinction brings up a couple of nuances. Traditional applications need to be designed and developed in such a way that they can take advantage of capabilities provided by the cloud platform, be it at the PaaS layer or IaaS layer. Even if a traditional application runs on the cloud, it is still based on the old tenets of compute-limited software design. Applications designed specifically for the cloud will perform better in the cloud than those that are adapted to a cloud model.

Cloud-centric or born-on-the-cloud applications should be developed

- to take advantage of cloud computing features such as scalability, which is the ability to handle additional workloads in the future, and elasticity, which is the ability to dynamically add resources or give back resources according to demand;

- using the new breed of tools and runtimes that are more nimble and dynamic;

- with constant change and upgrade in mind, using a DevOps approach; and

- to operate in a multi-tenant model

Adapting and developing services for the cloud does not mean all traditional apps and tools have to be abandoned. However, new rules of application design must be followed. Application isolation, security, and scalability have to be kept in mind when adapting traditional apps to take advantage of the cloud delivery model. These apps need to run without colliding with other apps in the shared infrastructure and should not break. Additionally, cloud application designers and developers should keep in mind that there is a strong requirement these days for mobile support for most customer-facing applications.

Cloudlets

In addition to the cloud terms discussed in this chapter, you may hear references to *community cloud,* which is a collaborative effort between several organizations to share infrastructure and resources. And you probably have heard that there are three basic types of cloud solutions: private cloud, public cloud, and hybrid cloud. The public cloud uses primarily IaaS. PaaS lends itself to private clouds, but it is moving to public clouds as well.

To quote an IBM executive, there are three business objectives that the cloud enables:

- Speed: enterprises can quickly obtain IT resources.

- Economics: capital expenditures are minimized.

- Empowerment: developers and users can access computing resources when needed.

One customer who has adopted cloud computing says, "We no longer plan for capacity because we have capacity on demand." Another observes, "Cloud is not just about infrastructure; it allows us to use ready-made applications in a cost-effective manner."

Of course, not everything about the cloud is rosy. IT architects face challenges regarding the lack of standardization, and CIOs need to consider whether a particular cloud service provider will still be in business five years from now. Nevertheless, in 2012 Gartner predicted that by 2016, 80 percent of Fortune 1000 enterprises will use some cloud computing services, and 20 percent of business will own no IT assets at all. Cloud computing and IT security remain at the top of the list of key priorities for 2015-2016 identified by IT decision-makers in Peak 10's annual U.S. market survey. And Forrester Research forecasts that the global market for cloud computing will grow to more than $241 billion by 2020.

2

Pure Platform in the Cloud

O f the three service layers in the cloud, Infrastructure as a Service (IaaS), Platform as a Service (PaaS), and Software as a Service (SaaS), PaaS is the most interesting because of its overlap with IaaS and its unavoidable encroachment into SaaS. Although it attempts to hide the complexities of IaaS, PaaS lays bare the challenges with the software that runs on the platform. PaaS at its most basic level is compute nodes running a particular operating system and some middleware in a particular topology. The challenges arise from the need to integrate various back-end systems.

Enterprises are under constant pressure to reduce costs and increase profits, and business units want IT to provide information faster, easier, and cheaper. That is where the IBM PureSystems® family of computer systems comes in. These systems are designed to deliver value through three core attributes:

- Built-in expertise—The PureSystems line is a new breed of computers known as *expert integrated systems,* or *converged systems,* which help address business and operational tasks by automating many of the manual steps in building cloud systems, thus reducing the cost of support and maintenance of the systems.

- Integration by design—All hardware and software components contained in these systems are integrated and optimized in the lab for increased performance and efficiency.

- Simplified experience—PureSystems also eliminates the need to procure, deploy, manage, and support various components separately, thereby providing built-in efficiencies.

The IBM PureApplication® system, shown in Figure 2.1, is a private-cloud platform for enterprise applications. It is workload-aware, flexible, and designed for easy deployment. PureApplication allows middleware and related applications to be customized, managed, and monitored. The most current and detailed information about IBM PureApplication is available at the IBM knowledge center, *www-01.ibm.com/support/knowledgecenter/SSCR9A_2.1.0/pv_welcome.html*.

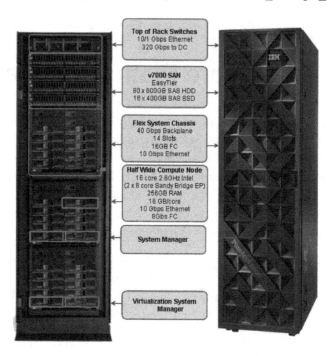

Figure 2.1: IBM PureApplication system

This chapter presents IBM PureApplication as the cloud computing platform and sets the stage for an architecture overview in Chapter 3.

Resources in PureApplication

Figure 2.2 illustrates the components of PureApplication. The three basic components—compute, networking, and storage—are integrated and optimized. Virtualization across the stack facilitates development, deployment, and unified management of not only the computing resources and middleware but of all the enterprise applications that require high performance, scalability, and optimal resource usage.

Figure 2.2: PureApplication building blocks

Like all other private cloud platforms, PureApplication contains both hardware resources and cloud resources. Table 2.1 lists those resources.

Table 2.1: PureApplication system resources

Hardware Resources	Cloud Resources
Compute nodes	IP addresses
Management nodes	IP groups
Storage devices	Cloud groups
Network devices	Environment profiles
External access networks	Virtual machines
Top-of-rack switches	Storage volumes
	Virtual appliances

The relationship diagram in Figure 2.3 illustrates the relationship between hardware resources (Compute Node, Virtual Machine, and Storage Volume) and cloud resources (the middle and left areas of the diagram). An IP group can contain one or more IP addresses, and a cloud group can have one or more IP groups. A user group contains many users. One or more environment profiles can be associated with users or user groups.

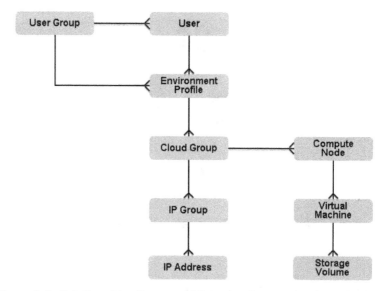

Figure 2.3: Relationship diagram of PureApplication system resources

Multiple storage volumes can be attached to a virtual machine (VM), and one or more VMs are associated with a cloud group. Thus, VMs are deployed on the compute node or nodes that are part of the cloud group. To better manage storage volumes, you can create storage volume groups to a cloud group.

To be able to work with hardware resources, you must have one or more of the following authorization levels:

- **System** level, **Hardware** administration role with **Full** permission to **Manage** hardware resources to view and manage all compute node instances

- **System** level, **Hardware** administration role with permission to **View** all hardware resources (Read-only)

- **Resource**-level administration role with **Write** or **All** access rights permission to view and manage a specific instance

- **Resource**-level administration role with **Read** access rights permission to view a specific instance

Let's look at the highlights of what these resources do and how to work with them in PureApplication. For detailed specifications, you can refer to any IBM Redbook on the topic at *www.redbooks.ibm.com.*

Compute Nodes

A compute node consists of a combination of microprocessors, memory, and Ethernet controllers. The components receive power and network connections from the chassis. The number of VMs that can be deployed on a compute node depends on the virtual CPU (vCPU) and memory allocations for the VMs. If sufficient storage is available, IBM PureApplication deploys to the compute nodes until either the vCPU or the memory resource is exhausted.

Management Nodes

Management nodes manage the PureApplication compute nodes. There are two management nodes: PureSystems Manager and the Virtualization System Manager. There are two of each type of management node on a rack.

Storage Devices

A PureApplication system contains a pair of IBM Storwize® V7000 storage units, each of which is a controller node paired with an expansion node, clustered with one controller managing both units as a single storage area network (SAN). The disks in the V7000 unit are the primary storage devices on the PureApplication system. There are a few solid-state drives, but most are hard disk drives, each with 0.5 GB of storage.

Top-of-Rack Switches

A top-of-rack switch is the gateway into the customer's network. PureApplication contains a pair of Lenovo RackSwitch™ G8264 64-port 10 Gb Ethernet switches. Systems administrators can physically access these switches from the rear of the rack or view the user interface via the system console. When you go to **System Console**

> Hardware > Network Devices, the page lists each chassis' network and SAN switches. The network administrator can see details about the network configuration by going to **System Console > System > Customer Network Configuration**.

IP Groups

PureApplication accesses IP addresses through IP groups. An IP group is a list or range of IP addresses that you can select to then use with specific VMs. IP groups provide a way to achieve isolation. For example, you could split 100 IP addresses into four blocks of 25 IP addresses each to be used by four departments in your enterprise. Even though these IP addresses are all on the same real subnet, creating the IP groups enables you to isolate them and thus the deployed instances.

PureApplication uses all available IP addresses from an IP group. During the deployment process, VMs continue to be assigned IP addresses until the IP group runs out of addresses.

Cloud Groups

A cloud group is the most fundamental concept that lets you use resources while maintaining separation, and hence security. A cloud group is a logical grouping of computing resources (i.e., compute nodes), and each cloud group requires one or more compute nodes and one or more IP groups. VMs are deployed on the compute nodes that are part of a chosen cloud group.

Cloud groups organize compute nodes and IP groups. There are two types of cloud groups: Dedicated and Average. These type definitions define how resources are allocated to a VM during deployment. Table 2.2 shows the breakdown of resources for the two types of cloud groups. Note the differences between Intel-based and IBM Power–based architectures.

 Note: The Average setting provides a 4:1 ratio of virtual CPUs. For example, if a compute node has 16 physical cores, an Average setting yields 64 vCPUs. The Dedicated setting gives a 1:1 ratio of vCPUs to physical cores.

Table 2.2: Defined cloud groups with CPU and memory mapping

Type	Dedicated		Average	
	Power	Intel	Power	Intel
Physical cores per compute node	32	16	32	16
vCPUs per compute node	28	16	280	128
Maximum vCPUs per VM	28	16	64	32
Memory over commit	No	No	No	No
CPU count (1 vCPU)	1 physical core	1 physical core	Min 0.1 physical core	Min 0.125 physical core
Virtual memory (1 MB)	1 physical MB	1 physical MB	1 physical MB	1 physical MB

The PureApplication system manages the placement of VMs on the compute nodes within a cloud group. The cloud group may move VMs between compute nodes for load balancing or failover purposes. One or more compute nodes within a cloud group can also be designated for high availability.

Environment Profiles

Environment profiles provide specific configurations that are used when deploying workloads. You create environment profiles by grouping deployment-related items, such as VM names, IP address assignments, and cloud groups. Environment profiles are platform-specific, so you can use them to deploy a workload to multiple cloud groups of the same hypervisor type.

Because environment profiles define the policies for how patterns are deployed on cloud groups, creating them correctly is essential to facilitating and managing deployments and running instances. In other words, environment profiles logically isolate the allocated resources, keeping application environments such as development, test, and production environments separate. Isolation prevents users and groups from using up more resources than they are allocated.

Figure 2.4 depicts how physical and logical isolation of resources within the PureApplication system is achieved using compute nodes, environment profiles (EP), cloud groups (CG), and IP groups (IPG). Resource isolation allows IT teams to create different application environments to which workloads can be deployed and managed within a PureApplication system. The recommendation is to use Average cloud groups in lower-level environments such as development and test environments, and to use Dedicated cloud groups in higher-level environments such as performance and production.

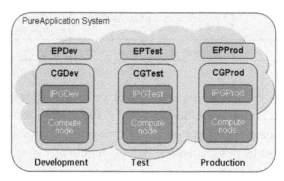

Figure 2.4: Application environments in the PureApplication system

Virtual Machines

When you successfully deploy resources, you get an instance of a VM. You can connect directly to the VM console of a deployed virtual system, but you need a special IP group, called an MKS Console IP group, to help you connect to that remote console. The MKS Console IP group must contain enough IP addresses to assign one to each compute node in the system.

 Tip: Make sure that ports 443, 902, and 903 are open for the IP addresses you define in the IP group to avoid network connectivity problems.

Users and User Groups

Users are created so they can access certain parts of the PureApplication system. By assigning special permissions to users, you can manage the level of access each user has. For management purposes, you can combine users into user groups by assigning different permissions to each group.

Getting Started with PureApplication

If you have access to a PureApplication system and the required credentials, you can bring up the Web-based user interface in a Web browser. The systems administrator should have provided you with the URL or IP address.

Figure 2.5 shows the initial login screen. You have to enter the username and password and click **Log In**. Notice that the name and serial number of the selected system or rack appear at the bottom of the login window.

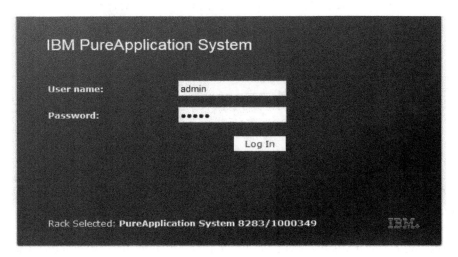

Figure 2.5: PureApplication system login screen

Once logged in, you'll see the welcome screen to the workload console. If you have additional system-level permissions, you will also see the system console shown in Figure 2.6. The system console is for system-level tasks such as creating IP groups and cloud groups and adding users, while the workload console is where you work with images, deploy patterns and workloads, and view VM instances.

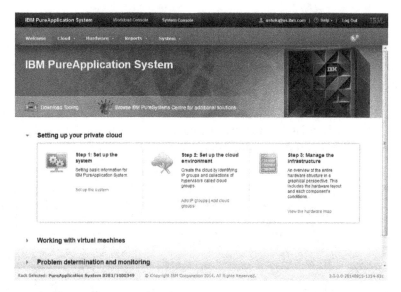

Figure 2.6: PureApplication system welcome screen

Although the system and workload consoles look very similar, there are slight differences in the main menus and sub-menus, as Table 2.3 shows. There is some overlap, but pattern developers and deployers will primarily use the workload console and hardware, and system administrators will work mostly with the system console options.

Table 2.3: PureApplication console menus and sub-menus

Workload Console		System Console	
Menu	Sub-menus	Menu	Sub-menus

Welcome	Working with virtual applications
	Working with virtual systems
	Onboarding existing applications
	  into the cloud
		Welcome	Setting up your private cloud
			Working with virtual machines
			Problem determination and
			  monitoring

Instances	All instances
	  Virtual Applications
	Virtual Systems
	Virtual Systems (classic)
	Virtual Machines
	Shared Services
		Cloud	IP Groups
			  Cloud Groups
			Virtual Appliances
			Virtual Machines
			Virtual Machine Groups
			Storage Volumes
			Storage Volume Groups

Patterns	Virtual Applications Virtual Systems Virtual Systems (classic)	Hardware	Infrastructure Map Compute Nodes Management Nodes Storage Devices Network Devices Network Topology Flex Chassis
Catalog	Reusable Components Components Definition Virtual Application Templates Virtual System Templates Virtual Images Script Packages Add-Ons IBM Installation Manager Repository Emergency Fixes DB2 Fix Packs (Virtual Systems) Database Images (Virtual Systems) Database Tools	Reports	Machine Activity User Activity Metering Chargeback IP Usage License Usage

Cloud	Shared Services
	System Plug-Ins
	Pattern Types
	Default Deploy Settings
	Environment Profiles
		System	Auditing
			Settings
			System Maintenance
			Users
			User Groups
			Security
			Network Configuration
			Management Domain
			  Configuration
			Job Queue
			Events
			Troubleshooting
			File Viewer
			Problems Block Storage
			  Replication
			Product Licenses

Table 2.3: PureApplication console menus and sub-menus

| Workload Console | | System Console | *Continued* |
Menu	Sub-menus	Menu	Sub-menus
System	Troubleshooting File Viewer Storehouse Browser Key Manager Adapters		

Download Tooling	Download command-line tool
	Download IBM Workload Plug-in
	    Development kit
	Download IBM Image Construction
	    and Composition Tool
	Download IBM Workload Deployer
	    Monitoring Agent Application
	    Support
		Download Tooling	Download command-line tool
			Download IBM PureApplication
			    System Monitoring Agent
			System Montoring Agent

Tip: Access to the consoles on PureApplication is controlled at the group level or at the user level. Systems administrators and others will have access to the system console, while developers and those who work with workloads will have access to the workload console.

Next, you need to complete a few basic configuration tasks. Before you can deploy a workload, you need to define an IP group, a cloud group, and an environment profile.

IP groups and cloud groups are visible in the system console; environment profiles fall in the workload console. The person who manages the PureApplication system will typically have created IP groups and cloud groups and mapped them to an environment profile that developers and workload deployers use. So if you have access to the workload console, you will have only read access to IP groups and cloud groups and won't be able to create them.

The next few screen captures are from an IBM Power-based PureApplication system, but you won't notice a difference. The PureApplication user experience is the same whether the platform is Intel-based, Power-based, or PureApplication Service on SoftLayer®, which is discussed in Chapter 9.

Working with IP Groups

To see the IP groups on the system, click Cloud on the system console and choose IP Groups. Highlighting a group displays the details in the main window, including all the IP addresses that are allotted to the group. Figure 2.7 shows an IP group named pas02-grp. The right pane lists the details for that group, including the virtual LAN (VLAN) ID and IP addresses.

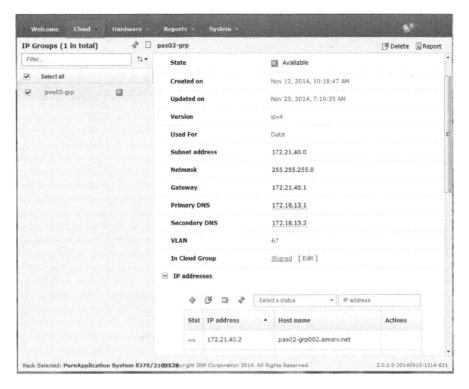

Figure 2.7: IP group information

 Note: VLANs are used for logical network isolation. When there are multiple VLANs on the same physical network, VLAN IDs allow data to be routed to specific VLANs

Should you have the opportunity to create a new IP group, you would click the **New** icon and fill in all the information shown in Figure 2.8. After providing a name, you need to work with the network administrator to obtain the DNS and VLAN information necessary to enter the networking details. In most cases, you'll select **Data** for the **Used For** field, the other option being **Management**.

Figure 2.8: Creating a new IP group

 Tip: Develop a naming convention for all cloud resources you create. For example, you might prefix IP group names with *ipg*, cloud group names with *cg*, and environment profiles with *ep*.

After you click **OK** and the new IP group is created, you can add the range of IP addresses that will be part of that group. Then you can make the IP group part of a cloud group.

Working with Cloud Groups

In the system console, click the **Cloud** tab and choose **Cloud Groups**. When Pure-Application is set up, a default cloud group named Shared is typically created. In Figure 2.9 you can see that Shared contains the IP group pas02-grp that was created earlier and the two compute nodes on the rack.

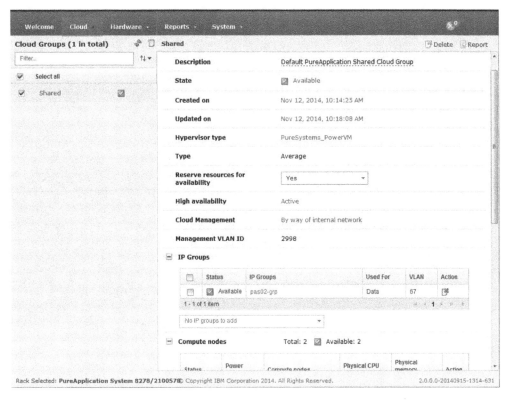

Figure 2.9: Cloud group information

To create a new cloud group, you would click the **New** icon and fill in all the information shown in Figure 2.10. After naming the cloud group, you would choose Average or Dedicated for the type. In most cases, cloud management is allowed to use the internal network and you need to supply a management VLAN ID. After you click **OK** to create the cloud group, you can configure the group to add one or more IP groups and one or more compute nodes.

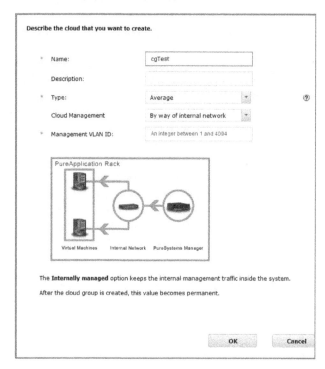

Figure 2.10: Creating a new cloud group

Some security-conscious enterprises might want to route connections via an external network. In this case you would choose the **By way of external network** option in the **Cloud Management** field. That option sends all network traffic outside the system so it can be monitored and controlled through the company's firewall. The graphic that's displayed in that case illustrates the routing, as Figure 2.11 shows.

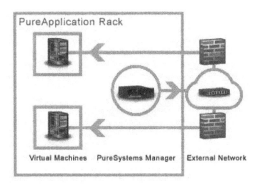

Figure 2.11: External routing of cloud group network connections

Working with Environment Profiles

The final resource you need before you can deploy anything is an environment profile. In the workload console, go to the Cloud menu and choose Environment Profiles. If an environment profile exists, it will be listed, and highlighting it will display the details in the main window, as in Figure 2.12. Among other things, you can set the deployment priority, time zone, and language. The deployment priority options are Platinum, Golden, Silver, and Bronze, and each category has an associated setting. You will also see the cloud group to which the environment profile is mapped.

Figure 2.12: Environment profile information

Environment profiles provide configuration information that's used when deploying a pattern. You can even specify an environment with multiple clouds and configure specific resources within that cloud. Customers often set up separate profiles for different environments, such as development, test, and production environments. To create a new environment profile, you would click the **New** icon and fill in the needed information, as shown in Figure 2.13. After choosing the profile type and describing the environment, click **OK** to create the profile, which you can then associate with one or more cloud groups.

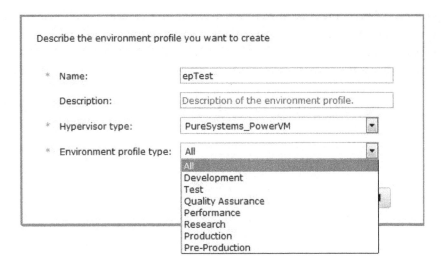

Figure 2.13: Creating a new environment profile

Now that you have all the pieces, you're ready to deploy a pattern. But what is a pattern, and where can you obtain one? This will be explianed shortly, but first you need to understand virtual images.

Virtual Images

Virtual images are Open Virtualization Format–compliant images. In PureApplication, virtual images have activation logic to assist in deployment. IBM software products specifically produce Hypervisor Edition (HVE) images. HVE images contain parts of virtual system patterns. You'll find HVE image files packaged as Open Virtualization Archive (OVA) files, which can be imported into the virtual image catalog in PureApplication.

These virtual images provide the operating system and product binary files required to create a virtual system instance. Certain virtual images, such as operating system images and WebSphere® Application Server images, come preinstalled on the PureApplication system. Intel-based PureApplication systems come with the IBM OS Image for Red Hat® Linux® Systems virtual image, and Power-based PureApplication comes with the IBM OS Image for AIX Systems, as you can see in Figure 2.14. These images can be extended to customize the virtual images and the operating system. You can also transform your own certified OS into an image that PureApplication can deploy. This can be done using the IBM Image Construction and Composition Tool (ICCT), which is available as part of the PureApplication Tooling.

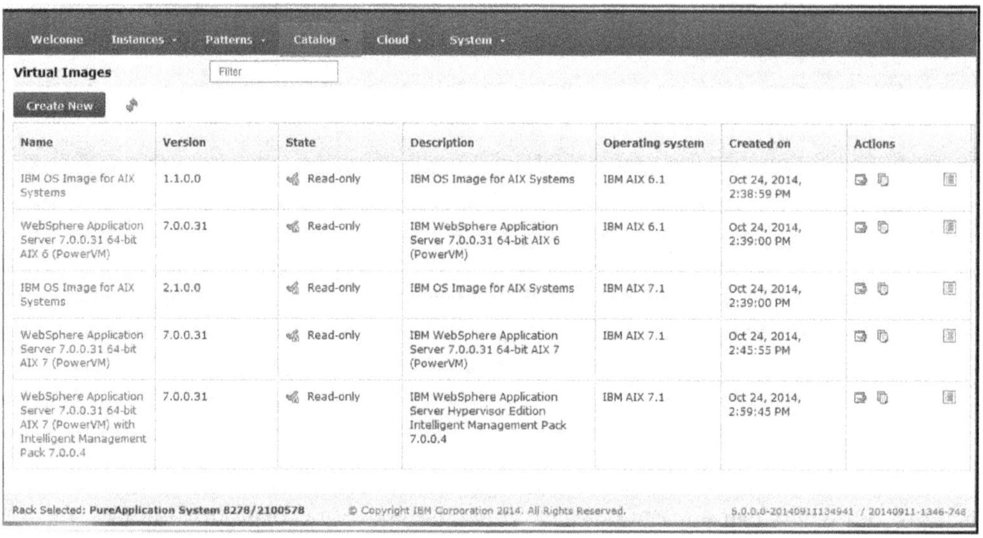

Figure 2.14: Virtual images on a Power-based PureApplication system

HVE images contain parts, which are various elements of particular software, such as middleware. For example, the IBM WebSphere Application Server HVE image includes the deployment manager, custom nodes, IBM HTTP Server, administrative agents, job manager, on-demand routers, and even a standalone server. These elements are visible when you highlight an image. Figure 2.15 shows the parts of the WebSphere Application Server 7.0.0.31 64-bit AIX 7 image and the assembled patterns.

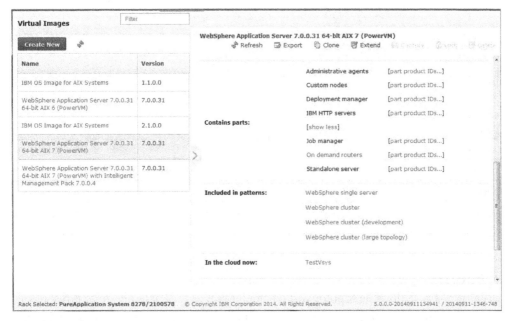

Figure 2.15: Details of the WebSphere Application Server hypervisor image

Figure 2.15 also shows a list of functions and actions at the top of the pane and a list of patterns included in the pattern. A few of the actions are grayed out for various reasons. For example, the Delete action is not available because the resource is in use. The Lock action is not available because you can't enable write permissions on a read-only resource.

Table 2.4 describes the functions and actions that can be performed on virtual images. The patterns can range from a single server to a cluster to a highly available topology. These variations are described in the next section on patterns.

Table 2.4: Available functions and actions for virtual images

Functions/Actions	Description
Refresh	Refreshes the status of the virtual image
Export	Exports a virtual image that can be imported into another system
Clone	Creates an exact copy
Extend	Creates an exact copy and allows you to extend it
Capture	Captures a deployed image
Lock	Configures the virtual image as read-only and prevents further editing
Delete	Deletes the virtual image
Create New	Brings up a window for OVA file information, which can be imported to create a new image

Patterns

A pattern is a deployable topology of particular software. There are three types of patterns meant for each cloud service layer: infrastructure patterns, platform patterns, and application patterns. These virtualized patterns offer efficient, automated, and repeatable deployment of software systems that include VM instances and the middleware or applications that run on them. For example, if we were to deploy the WebSphere single-server pattern shown in Figure 2.15, there would be a single VM instance running a standalone WebSphere Application Server.

If you go back to the virtual images screen (from the workload console, click **Catalog > Virtual Images**) and choose **WebSphere Application Server 7.0.0.31 64-bit**, then click the **WebSphere single server pattern** link, you're taken to the details page of that classic virtual system pattern, shown in Figure 2.16.

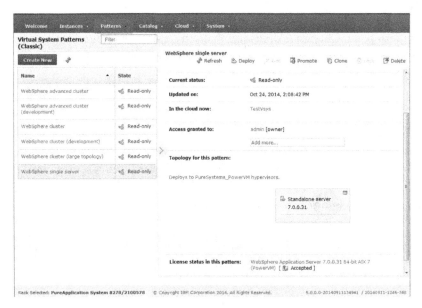

Figure 2.16: Details of the WebSphere single-server pattern

The screen also shows pattern-related functions and actions. Some actions, such as Promote, are unique to classic virtual system patterns. Table 2.5 describes the functions and actions that can be performed on patterns.

Table 2.5: Functions and actions available for classic virtual system patterns

Functions/Actions	Description
Refresh	Refreshes the status of the virtual image
Deploy	Creates a running instance of the pattern
Edit	Opens the pattern for editing within the pattern editor
Promote	Promotes the pattern to use the monitoring, logging, and other tools available to V2 patterns
Clone	Creates an exact copy of the pattern to let you create a new one
Lock	Sets the status of the pattern to Read-only preventing it from further modification
Delete	Deletes the pattern from the PureApplication System
Create New	Creates a new pattern

You can now deploy a pattern, which is as simple as clicking the Deploy icon on the pattern pane. Chapter 3 dives into pattern deployment and discusses patterns in more detail. But before we continue, let's look at the infrastructure map in the PureApplication system console.

The Infrastructure Map

The infrastructure map is one of the most interesting screens in the PureApplication user interface. To display a map of the system hardware, go to the system console, then select **Infrastructure Map** under **Hardware**. You'll see a screen similar to Figure 2.17. If you don't want the serial numbers to be displayed, toggle the **Show Component Name** button to hide the legend on the left.

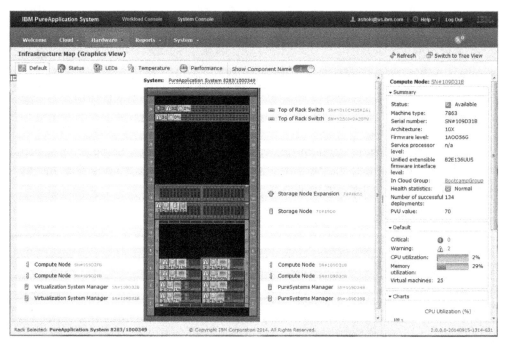

Figure 2.17: PureApplication system infrastructure map

The hardware map displays near-real-time status of all hardware components in the rack—the top-of-rack switches, storage nodes, compute nodes, and the PureSystem and virtualization system managers. If you click any component in the graphic display, the details of that component are displayed in the right pane.

Figure 2.17 shows the details of the top right compute node, which has the serial number 109D31B. You can see the status of the component, its health, and its utilization statistics. And you can see that this particular resource, the compute node, belongs to the cloud group named BootcampGroup.

Cloudlets

The newest release of PureApplication, V2.1, has adopted the mega menu style for the console user interface. A mega menu is a big, two-dimensional drop-down panel that groups navigation options to eliminate scrolling and uses typography, icons, and tooltips to explain users' choices. Figure 2.18 shows the options under the new Patterns menu. While the new user interface has all the same console menu options as before, there is no longer the top-level split of Workload Console and System Console.

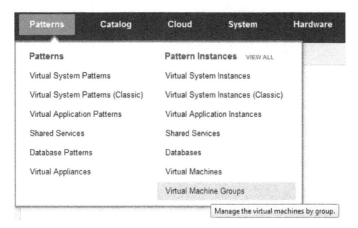

Figure 2.18: Patterns menu in PureApplication V2.1

The cloud platform enables the efficient use of hardware resources and cloud resources, such as IP groups and VMs. A lot goes on under the covers, but the beauty of the cloud, at least from a user's perspective, is that all that complexity is hidden. The cloud consumer simply wants to be able to deploy software, use an app, or access resources without having to worry about how things are run or managed. The PureApplication system, which is an on-premises or private cloud platform, does exactly that, hiding the computing complexities. You simply specify the workload you want to deploy, and the contained pattern engine takes care of the rest. And that ultimately is the promise of the cloud.

References

- PureApplication System Technote: *www-01.ibm.com/support/docview .wss?uid=swg21664644*

- IBM Redbook tip: *www.redbooks.ibm.com/abstracts/tips0959.html*

- WSO2 Private PaaS: *wso2.com/cloud/private-paas*

- Apache Stratos Project: *stratos.apache.org*

3

Cloud Software Patterns

A pattern is a predefined architecture of a product or application that has been tested, optimized, and captured in a deployable form. Patterns encapsulate installation and configuration best practices, are pre-integrated across components, and are preconfigured and tuned. Because a pattern is in a deployable form, you can deploy it repeatedly with identical results and full lifecycle management.

Patterns are not new to IT—we already have software design patterns and software architecture templates. Now we have software patterns in the cloud. These patterns are templates of software solutions that can be deployed repeatedly. They can be simple operating system virtual images or multi-tier enterprise solutions that are captured for future cloning and instantiation. IBM also has *patterns of expertise,* which are encapsulations of installation and configuration best practices of a single product or a solution-level topology. Whether you call them templates or recipes or patterns, the underlying notion is the same.

This chapter discusses patterns that are part of IBM's PureApplication platform. The term "platform" is used here because, thanks to the pattern engine, patterns can run in PureApplication System, PureApplication Service on SoftLayer, or Pure-Application Software. PureApplication patterns created by IBM or its business partners are available from the PureSystems Centre at *www.ibm.com/software/brand catalog/puresystems/centre.*

You deploy patterns with the help of a deployment engine or pattern engine, which provides the framework that helps choreograph an abstract representation into a virtualized system. A pattern that has been deployed as a usable system is called a *pattern instance.* The value of patterns lies in the fact that you can deploy many instances of the same pattern very easily. Figure 3.1 shows how a deployed topology maps to a pattern instance running in PureApplication.

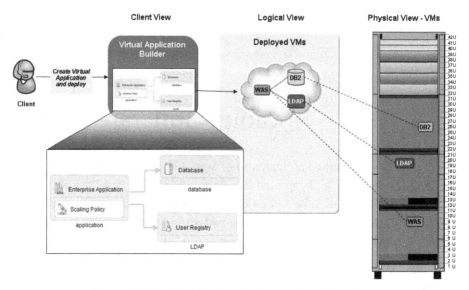

Figure 3.1: Logical to physical mapping of patterns

If there is a secret sauce in PureApplication, it's the built-in patterns and the hundreds of patterns available. There are three types of patterns, which correspond to the cloud service layers:

- Infrastructure patterns provide an automated, policy-driven infrastructure deployment and management approach across compute, storage, and networking resources. These patterns are designed to reduce operational expenses and increase performance by enabling faster configuration of hardware and simplifying low-level resource management.

- Platform patterns provide preconfigured and policy-managed platform services such as caching, elasticity, failover, load balancing, and security monitoring. Platform patterns enable faster and more efficient deployment and management to application services, databases, and messaging middleware.

- Application patterns provide predefined application architecture and required platform services that the system deploys and manages according to a set of policies. Application patterns help build robust, scalable, and easily maintained solutions for various architectures.

Patterns are further differentiated based on how they are built—specifically, according to the amount of exposure to the underlying virtual machines (VMs). Virtual system patterns, commonly called vSys patterns, give users total access to the deployed virtual machines. These patterns provide automated, policy-driven infrastructure deployment and management across compute, storage, and networking resources. vSys patterns reduce operational expenses and improve performance by enabling faster configuration of hardware and simplifying low-level resource management. Figure 3.2 shows the components that go into the composition of a virtual system pattern and the contents of such an instance when it's deployed.

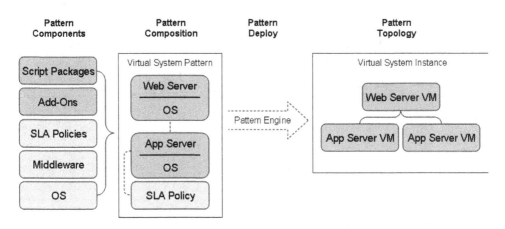

Figure 3.2: Virtual system patterns

Virtual application (aka vApp) patterns operate at a higher level of abstraction, wherein either the VM is preconfigured or the customer provides his own enterprise-hardened VM, including policy-managed platform services such as caching, elasticity, failover, load balancing, and security monitoring. Using these services, platform patterns enable faster and more efficient deployment and management to application services, database, and messaging middleware.

39

Both vSys and vApp patterns supplement the activities of installation, configuration, and integration of software and assist IT personnel in accomplishing and managing their tasks. The patterns are nested within the activities with which they interact. In vSys patterns, scripts store the messages that are passed between the activities and partners, or components. In vApp patterns, plug-ins fill that role. Figure 3.3 shows the progression of a virtual system pattern to a virtual application pattern via the inclusion of custom components, and shows the content of the deployed instance.

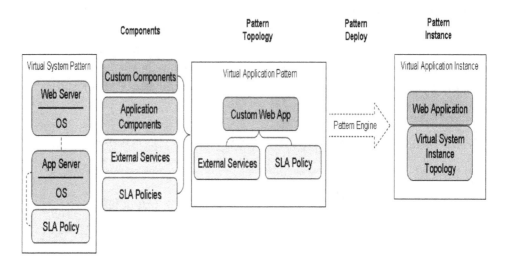

Figure 3.3: Virtual application patterns

Working with Patterns

Let's look now at how to work with patterns. Regardless of the type of pattern, you benefit from treating a potentially complex middleware infrastructure environment or middleware application as a single unit throughout its lifecycle of creation, deployment, and management. For example, most companies have business processes and use a business process management product. Setting up business processes takes a lot of time and effort, and using a pattern for that purpose cuts the time significantly and makes the job much easier. The pattern used for the examples in this section is the IBM Business Process Manager (BPM) pattern. Because the BPM environment is rather complex to set up, the BPM pattern is one of the most commonly requested and used patterns on the PureApplication platform. You can learn a lot from looking at the BPM pattern in detail.

 Note: The BPM pattern discussed here is the Virtual System (Classic) pattern. This pattern best illustrates many virtualization concepts. Classic patterns are available and supported in both the old and new versions of PureApplication.

The BPM pattern is not a single pattern. The hypervisor image includes the BPM Advanced Clustered Pattern, BPM Advanced Clustered Process Center pattern, and BPM Advanced Clustered Process Server pattern.

You can check the catalog on the PureApplication workload console to see whether the rack has been loaded with the BPM pattern by clicking **Workload Console > Catalog > Virtual Images**. If the pattern hasn't been loaded, you can use an OVA image file to load it, a process known as *on-boarding* a pattern. You can also use supplied pattern parts to create your own patterns, as explained in Chapter 4, or even create a completely new pattern from scratch.

To upload the BPM pattern if it isn't already loaded on the PureApplication platform, you can use the command-line interface (CLI). Go to the main Pure-Application console, click the **Welcome** tab, and choose the **Download command line tool** option. Download the tool and unzip the executable to a folder, preferably C:\IBM\Deployer. Add that path to the system path variable, then use the CLI and the following command to install the executable on the system that has the image file:

```
installer –h <IPAS_HOST> –u <USER_NAME> –p <PASSWORD>
```

After the virtual image is uploaded, make sure it shows up in the cloud catalog. From the workload console, select **Catalog** and choose **Virtual Images**. You should see an entry for IBM Business Process Manager Advanced 8.5.0.1 RHEL 6 x64 (VMWare), as Figure 3.4 shows. You can use the filter field to narrow the search results.

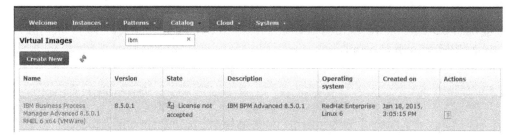

Figure 3.4: BPM virtual image loaded into PureApplication

Notice that the State column has a box containing a red **x** and says "License not accepted." The owner of the image must accept the license in order to activate the image. To accept the license, highlight the image and click **Accept** in the license agreement property. The Licenses screen will be displayed and will list one or more software components. Click each component and accept each license to change its icon to a green check mark. Figure 3.5 shows that licenses have been accepted for VMware Tools™ and IBM BPM Advanced License but not yet for Red Hat® Enterprise Linux® (RHEL). When finished, click **OK**.

Figure 3.5: Accepting licenses of virtual image software components

Tip: Licensing, Metering, and Chargeback are useful features provided by Cloud Platforms.

Now you can deploy the BPM pattern. In the workload console, under **Patterns**, choose **Virtual Systems (Classic)**. You'll see IBM BPM Advanced Clustered Process Server Pattern 8.5.0.1. Highlight it to see the details of the pattern in the main pane, or canvas. Notice that the **In the cloud now** field has a value of **none** because the pattern has not yet been deployed. If you scroll down, you can view the topology of the pattern, as Figure 3.6 shows. The five boxes denote the VMs in the pattern. You can change the numeral 2 at the top left corner of the **Process Server custom nodes** box to increase the number of nodes before initiating deployment. Increasing the number of nodes thus enables the platform to allow for vertical scaling.

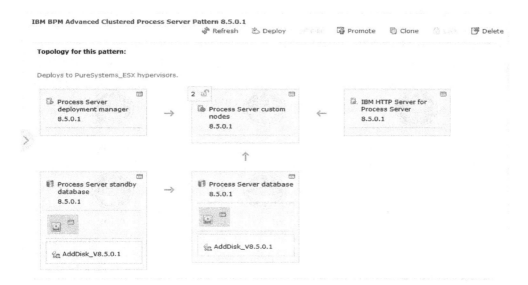

Figure 3.6: IBM BPM Advanced Clustered Process Server Pattern topology

Although only the BPM Advanced Clustered Process Server Pattern is discussed here, the BPM Advanced Clustered image also supports other system patterns.

- The BPM Advanced Clustered Pattern contains a Process Center and a Process Server environment, each with its respective database. These environments are fully clustered, production-ready topologies complete with Deployment Manager and fronted by a Web server. The database is DB2® and the Web server is IBM HTTP Server.

- The Process Center Pattern serves as a shared repository for a team. It contains a playback server that is heavily used during development of business process applications, as well as remote messaging and remote support environments spread over multiple VMs.

- The Process Server Pattern serves as the runtime environment. This fully clustered pattern is used to run business process applications during testing, staging, and production. It also contains remote messaging and remote support environments spread over multiple VMs, and it can run in both online and offline modes.

Deploying the BPM Pattern

Now you're ready to deploy your first pattern. Highlight the **BPM Advanced Clustered** pattern and select **Deploy in the cloud** from the menu at the top of the canvas. Enter a unique virtual system name, choose the environment or cloud group, and then configure the parts.

As Figure 3.7 shows, there are four virtual parts in the BPM Process Center and Process Server patterns: the custom nodes, the database, the Web server, and the deployment manager. Technically, the standby database is also considered to be a part. When you name the virtual system, choose a name that makes it easy to identify your pattern instance and the environment. When choosing the environment, you can also select the IP version of the environment and the cloud group. You can schedule an immediate deployment unless another deployment is in process. Finally, you configure the virtual parts.

The difference between the parts of a Process Center pattern and a Process Server pattern is not only their prefixes, but also their properties. Figure 3.8 shows the properties for the Process Server deployment manager part (BPMPSDMGRPart).

Figure 3.7: Virtual parts in the BPM pattern

Figure 3.8: Properties of Process Server deployment manager part

Each part has certain common properties that need to be configured, such as virtual CPUs and memory size. It is recommended that you begin with one virtual CPU and a memory size of 3072; if necessary, you can increase these values later. As the deployer, you select the BPM administrative username and password, which are needed to connect to the BPM consoles. If you want to maintain the process server offline, do not enter the Process Center connection details; otherwise, specify the correct Process Center URL, username, and password.

Tip: When creating an offline Process Server, it's helpful to include "Offline" in the name of the part, as in Figure 3.8, for easier identification.

Table 3.1 lists the number of VMs that are created by default when the BPM pattern is deployed. As mentioned earlier, the actual number will vary depending on how many custom nodes are chosen.

Table 3.1: Default number of VMs in the BPM Virtual System classic pattern

	Web Server	Database	Deployment Manager	Custom Nodes	Total
Process Center pattern	1	1+1	1	2	6
Process Server pattern	1	1+1	1	2	6
					12

As you see in Figure 3.8, the other parts in the pattern are the Process Server custom nodes, IBM HTTP Server for Process Server, the Process Server database, and the Process Server standby database. Figure 3.9 shows the properties for the BPM Process Server custom node part (BPMPSCustomNodePart). Again, you select the number of virtual CPUs and the memory size. After you enter all values, click OK.

Similarly, you need to fill in values for the Process Server database part, which includes a disk size. After all parameter values for all the parts are filled in, you'll see green check marks by all the pattern components. Clicking **OK** kicks off the

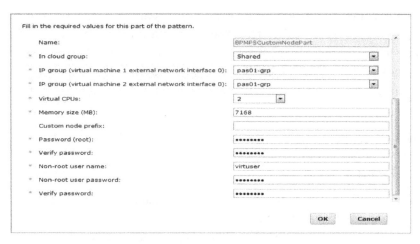

Fill in the required values for this part of the pattern.

Name:	BPMPSCustomNodePart	
* In cloud group:	Shared	▼
* IP group (virtual machine 1 external network interface 0):	pas01-grp	▼
* IP group (virtual machine 2 external network interface 0):	pas01-grp	▼
* Virtual CPUs:	2	▼
* Memory size (MB):	7168	
Custom node prefix:		
* Password (root):	••••••••	
* Verify password:	••••••••	
* Non-root user name:	virtuser	
* Non-root user password:	••••••••	
* Verify password:	••••••••	

OK   Cancel

Figure 3.9: Properties of the Process Server custom node part

deployment process and brings up the instances screen—in this case, the Virtual System Instances (Classic) screen in Figure 3.10. You can access the instances screen by clicking **Workload Console > Instances > Virtual Systems Instances (Classic)**.

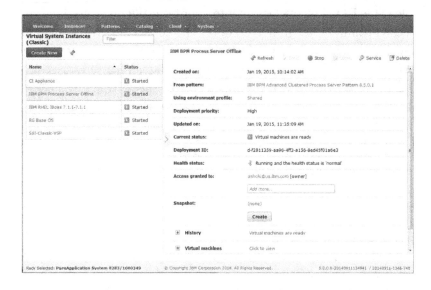

Figure 3.10: BPM Process Server instance details

The information on the instances screen includes the total number of VMs and the current status of the virtual system. The status is a cumulative status, so if there is a failure in any one part or any one script, the status indicates failure. An arrow in the green box next to BPM Process Server indicates a successful deployment. If there is a problem during deployment, a red circle will be displayed along with an error message.

The details pane shows the VMs' current status and health status. You can expand the virtual machines section to see individual details of all VMs that were spun up during deployment.

To see the entire deployment history, you can expand the History section. Systems administrators use this function to determine how long the deployment took, the resources being consumed, and the scripts that were executed.

After all those steps, the actual deployment is almost anticlimactic because the pattern includes known best practices and is fully optimized. Once the deployment process begins, there is not much to do other than wait for the result.

Working with the BPM Pattern Instance

When the BPM pattern instance is running successfully, it's business as usual. You can download the IBM Process Designer to your local Windows machine and use it. Or you can open IBM Integration Designer and connect to the Process Center in the cloud if you deployed the IBM BPM Process Center. You can even open the WebSphere Integrated Solutions Console and peek into all the software components that were configured: deployment environment, WebSphere Application Server clusters, application servers, nodes, service integration buses, messaging engines, and the data sources. It may be helpful to bookmark all the URLs.

Remember that you can use either the IP address or the fully qualified host name to bring up the WebSphere Integrated Solutions Console. You may have to add the fully qualified host names to your local hosts file depending on how your Pure-Application system is configured on the network.

Integrated Solutions Console

You'll find the link to the WebSphere Integrated Solutions Console, commonly known as the WebSphere administrative console, in the deployment manager VM. Select the BPM pattern instance (**Workload Console > Instances > Virtual**

Systems). In the details, you'll find a VM named *<Cloud_Group_Name>*-BPM PS DMGR-*<Instance_Name>*.

Click the plus sign in the canvas to expand the details page, then scroll down. You'll see the link to the WebSphere administrative console in the Consoles section as **WebSphere**. Click that link to bring up the WebSphere administrative console login page shown in Figure 3.11. This page should look familiar if you've worked with WebSphere Application Server. You'll see that the user ID and password are what you entered on the BPMPSDMGRPart screen. Also note that the URL contains the fully qualified host name of the deployment manager VM.

Figure 3.11: WebSphere Integrated Solutions Console screen via the DMgr VM instance

BPM-Related Consoles

The IBM HTTP Server (IHS) is configured as the proxy server in the BPM pattern, which means all HTTP traffic flows through port 80. If you highlight the BPM pattern instance (**Workload Console > Instances > Virtual Systems**) and look at the details, you'll find a VM with the name *<Cloud_Group_Name>*-BPM PS IHS-*<Instance_Name>*.

Click the plus sign in the canvas to expand it, and scroll down. You'll see links to the BPM consoles in the Consoles section, as in Figure 3.12.

Figure 3.12: Web server VM instance showing the consoles

 Tip: In the details of the VM, the fully qualified host name and IP address are listed in the **Network interface** field. Make a note of these. You can get to the consoles directly by using the URLs rather than bringing up the details page every time.

We've seen how to deploy a pattern using the IBM BPM Advanced Clustered Process Server Pattern as an example. Using the pattern reduces the time to configure and deploy a fully clustered BPM environment to a matter of hours. You can delete an instance and create a new one at any time, and a cloud administrator can clone or extend an existing topology, even of offline BPM Process Server production servers.

Virtual System Pattern

The latest version of PureApplication System is V2.1. The underlying principles of patterns and pattern deployment remain the same as in the earlier version, but there are some significant differences in the new version of the virtual system pattern. The older version of the pattern is called Virtual System Classic Pattern, whereas the new version is simply Virtual System Pattern, and the pattern editor is quite different between the versions. The classic pattern editor has two panes—assets on the left and the main canvas on the right—and three types of assets: parts, scripts, and add-ons. The new system pattern editor has three panes, with assets on the left, the main canvas in the middle, and the details on the right. And in the newer version, assets include images, scripts, software components, debug components, and other components.

The IBM BPM Pattern for PureApplication System V2 is a new pattern, not a classic pattern. You'll find it in the workload console under **Patterns > Virtual Systems**. There are 10 variations of the pattern, shown in Figure 3.13.

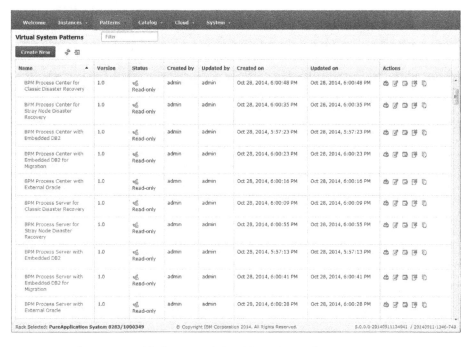

Figure 3.13: Variations of the BPM Virtual System Pattern

Let's use one variation to explore the user interface. Highlight **IBM Process Center with Embedded DB2**, and you'll see the details in the main canvas, as Figure 3.14 shows. Scroll down to see all the parts, scripts, and add-ons that make up the pattern along with the topology preview. You'll notice that where the classic pattern had boxes depicting VMs, the new pattern shows graphic images depicting machines with operating systems. When you hover over an icon in the thumbnail, the resources for that icon are displayed. The resources are grouped as software and scripts, add-ons, and policies.

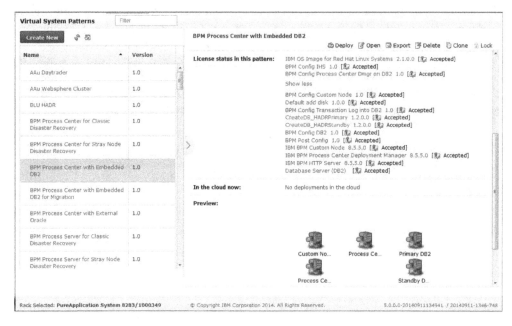

Figure 3.14: Details of the IBM Process Center pattern

The new pattern has the same action options as the classic pattern: Deploy, Open, Export, Delete, Clone, and Lock. To deploy this version of the IBM BPM pattern, just click **Deploy**. When the pattern deployment screen shown in Figure 3.15 appears, you can choose the environment profile, cloud group, and so on and make sure all the necessary information is entered in all the mandatory fields. Then click **Quick Deploy** to initiate the deployment process.

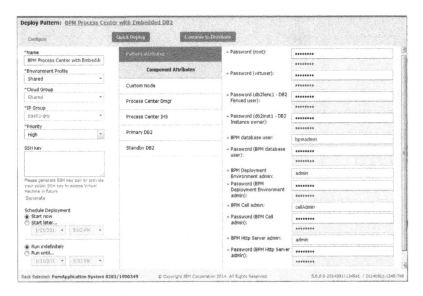

Figure 3.15: Virtual System Pattern deployment screen

To change the pattern topology or verify the contents of all the resources before deploying the pattern, click the **Open** action item. That brings up the new pattern editor or builder; Figure 3.16 shows the pattern builder.

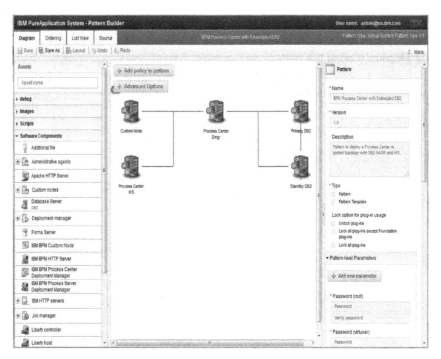

Figure 3.16: The new Virtual System Pattern builder

Notice all the assets in the left pane, the five VM topologies as originally designed in the pattern in the middle canvas, and the pattern configuration details in the right pane. When you highlight a VM, its particular details appear in the right pane. If you make changes in the editor, be sure to save your changes before deploying the pattern.

There's more than meets the eye with the new patterns and the pattern placement engine, but if something goes wrong you can always fall back to the default settings, which are optimized in each pattern. Remember that these patterns are pre-configured, tested, and tuned. For more information about the Virtual System Pattern, go to *wwwibm.com/developerworks/cloud/library/cl-puresystem-vsp/index.html.*

Tip: Quick Deploy deploys the pattern with the distribution and settings that were determined by the system. **Continue to Distribute** generates the pattern topology and placement recommendation for the pattern, which you, as the deployer, can customize before deployment.

Creating Patterns for Non-IBM Software

Thus far we've talked about and deployed patterns that were created from and for IBM software. Now let's tackle patterns for non-IBM software by going through the steps necessary to create a pattern for installing JBoss® Application Server on a VM running on IBM's PureApplication system. The requirements are

- An OS image must be available to use as the starting point.

- You must be able to download JBoss Application Server from *jbossas .jboss.org/downloads* and store it on your desktop.

- You must have permission to create PureApplication images and patterns.

In the workload console under the **Catalog** menu option, choose **Virtual Images**. You'll see all images currently available on PureApplication. Choose an OS image— the type of OS image will depend on whether you're using PureApplication System W2500, which is Intel-based, or PureApplication System W2700, which is Power-based. The following example uses an Intel-based system, so we'll use a Red Hat Linux image.

Highlight **IBM OS Image for Red Hat Linux Systems**, as in Figure 3.17. On the details page, you'll see options to Export, Clone, and Extend. Click **Extend**.

Figure 3.17: PureApplication system console showing virtual images

The message window shown in Figure 3.18 lets you know that a virtual system will be created that you can modify and capture as an image. Enter a unique name and a version number in the appropriate fields of the **General information** section. In the **Deployment configuration** section you can choose the environment profile and cloud group. You also need to provide a password, which you'll need later to modify the component. Click **OK**.

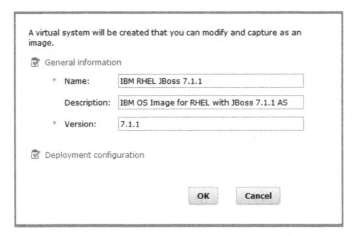

Figure 3.18: Virtual system creation information

It takes a few minutes to create the new system because the process starts up a new pattern instance. You can see the available hypervisor images by going to **Catalog > Virtual Images**. If you don't find the image you want, contact the PureApplication systems administrator.

 Tip: To prevent image sprawl, give others access to the image so they can use it, too.

For this example, the JBoss AS 7.1.1 TAR.GZ file was downloaded, as you can
see in Figure 3.19. The next step is to copy the JBoss binary to the VM instance
running on PureApplication. To securely log on to the instance, go to **Workload
Console > Instances > Virtual System Instances (Classic)**. You'll see a screen like
Figure 3.20 that shows the new instance that was created during the Extend operation. Scroll down to the **Virtual machines** section and click the **Log in** link to bring
up a Secure Shell (SSH) screen in a new Web browser window. The user ID to use is
root, and the password is the password you entered during the Extend operation.

| JBoss AS 7.1.1.Final | AS Certified Java EE 6 Full Profile | 2012-03-09 | LGPL | Community participation only | ZIP (127MB) Release Notes |
| | AS Certified Java EE 6 Full Profile | 2012-03-09 | LGPL | Community participation only | TAR.GZ (127MB) Release Notes |

Figure 3.19: JBoss application server download

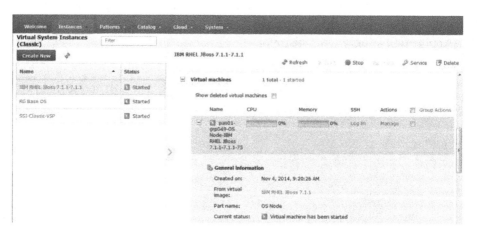

Figure 3.20: New instance details

A better way to open a command window on the deployed VM is to use a utility, such as Putty, that gives you more editing capabilities. Note that JBoss AS needs Java 1.6 or later. After you log on to the VM instance, you can run the command java -version to verify that Java is bundled in all OS instances on PureApplication System.

 Tip: To get the IP address of the VM, expand **Virtual machines** in the details pane of the VM and scroll down. The **Network interface** parameter value contains the fully qualified name of the VM and the IP address.

Create a folder named /opt/jboss. Now you can upload the JBoss .tgz binary to your VM instance using SCP or WinSCP. Alternatively, you can upload the RPM package of JBoss by using the rpm utility. RPM (RPM Package Manager) is a popular utility for installing software on UNIX-like systems, particularly Red Hat Linux. Since our example has the tar.gz file, we can "un-tar" it using the command

```
tar -zvxf jboss-as-7.1.1.Final.tar.gz
```

Go to the bin subfolder under /opt/jboss and run the standalone.sh command, preferably in the background, to start the JBoss application server. Verify that it's running by using the UNIX command

```
ps -aef | grep -i jboss
```

If you don't have Internet access from the VM instance, another way to verify that the startup was successful is to use the wget utility on a command line; for example:

```
wget http://localhost:8080
```

After entering the command, look for a response code of 200, which indicates success.

Now that you know the JBoss Application Server is running, the final step is to capture and save the image. In PureApplication's workload console, go to **Catalog > Virtual Images**. Highlight the newly minted image, which we named IBM RHEL JBoss 7.1.1. On the details page shown in Figure 3.21, you'll see three options on the top right: Capture, Lock, and Delete. Click **Capture**.

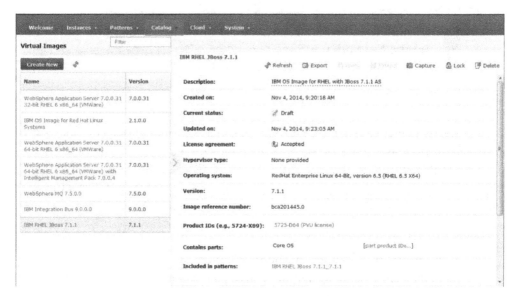

Figure 3.21: Option to capture an image

A message screen asks whether you really want to capture this virtual image and tells you that it will take some time to do so. Click **OK**. Eventually you'll see the image listed and its status changed from *Draft* to *Virtual image has been captured,* as in Figure 3.22. Now you can use the image to build other JBoss-related patterns. In this example, Extend and Capture was used to create a pattern for non-IBM software. Although that's a quick way to build an image for PureApplication, it is not the generally recommended approach because of ongoing maintenance requirements and the challenge of controlling the size of the image. A preferred alternative is to use scripts to install the software on an instantiated VM. Also, with this approach you must start the JBoss server manually. Writing a script package that starts the server upon deployment of the pattern would be a much better approach. In general, developing scripts and packaging them for use whenever you want to create such a pattern is the best option.

Figure 3.22: The image, captured!

Pattern Deployment for High Availability

One new feature of IBM PureApplication System V2 is the ability to spread pattern components across multiple PureApplication systems and cloud groups and thus achieve high availability. The first requirement is that you need a second Pure-Application System. Then you can create an environment profile that spans the two racks and deploy patterns across multiple systems. Cost efficiency is improved through replication of workloads and dynamic scaling across cloud groups and racks. PureApplication also provides a consolidated view of the pattern components and a single monitoring view of the deployed pattern across racks.

You need to create a management domain (**System Console > System > Management Domain Configuration**) so that the racks can share the catalog content, as illustrated in Figure 3.23. Note that before you create a management domain, you should define an externally managed IP address.

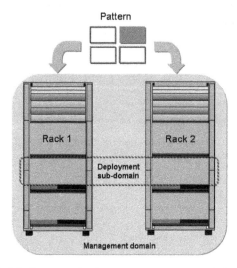

Figure 3.23: Pattern deployment across multiple systems

 Note: PureApplication systems within a domain can span any distance.

Then you can group systems within the domain into deployment subdomains and deploy a pattern across racks within a subdomain. Subdomains require low-latency connection between the systems.

Cloudlets

Patterns alleviate the guesswork and complexity of installing and configuring software, especially complex middleware. They allow users and developers to spend time on what they like to do—and do best—which is creating applications and testing them as and when needed before releasing them into production. Most out-of-the-box (OOB) patterns can be deployed as is. However, you should be aware that many patterns would need to be customized via scripts or custom deployment settings to fit into a client's required solution.

4

Scripting

Rather than remember all the commands necessary to perform a task or a series of tasks, IT professionals from the UNIX® world commonly collect the necessary commands in a file and save it. When read by the UNIX shell, the script file executes the embedded commands and makes it look as though the task was automated. A similar paradigm is useful when configuring IT resources in the cloud.

Nowadays a plethora of scripting languages act as interpreters, among them Node.js, Ruby, PHP, JavaScript, Perl, Jython, and Python. It is important to learn how to choose the appropriate scripting language to be used to create script packages that automate deployments and customize configurations in the cloud.

This chapter presents overviews and examples of some of the most popular scripting languages used with the cloud. It does not cover the various tools available to script developers, although later in the chapter we'll look at the wsadmin scripting utility.

Hello, Cloud Scripts

Every new scripting language tries to improve upon existing ones by offering simpler syntax or better error handling or simply by addressing a new and different need. How do you determine which scripting language to learn? The platform that you're working with is typically the primary consideration. If you plan to work on multiple platforms, you may want to choose and master a scripting language such as Python, which is available on every operating system.

Let's take the example of IBM's PureApplication System. On PureApplication, you can use the UNIX shell script (sh), Python, wsadmin, or a combination of the three. You could also embed cURL or Jython commands. On public cloud platform products such as Microsoft® Azure™, Heroku™ from Salesforce.com, and IBM's Bluemix™, we have to add Node.js and the variations of Ruby to the mix.

For those who are new to writing scripts or those who have used UNIX shell script commands in the past, here are some very simple scripts in various languages, most of which print "Hello Cloud," a twist on the traditional Hello World program. These examples are meant to jog your memory or act as a springboard to developing more meaningful and complex scripts.

 Tip: In most scripting languages, lines that start with a number or pound sign (#) are treated as comments.

Bash

```
#!/bin/bash
echo Hello Cloud
```

The first line of the UNIX shell script above tells the system which program to use to run the file. The second line is the only action performed by the script, which prints "Hello, Cloud" on the screen. If the file was saved under the name hello.sh, you would execute the file by entering the command

```
./hello.sh
```

PHP

```
<?php
Print "Hello, Cloud";
?>
 <?php
 Echo "Hello, Cloud";
 ?>
```

In PHP you can use either the Print or the Echo command. PHP runs on every platform and is a server-side scripting language, meaning that it's executed on the Web server.

Ruby

```
# My first Ruby program
puts 'Hello Cloud'
```

If you do not want to create a hellocloud.rb file, you can run the program using the following one-line command, which then prints the output shown.

```
$ ruby -e "puts 'Hello Cloud'"
Hello Cloud
```

You'll likely hear references to Ruby on Rails. Rails is an open-source Web application framework; Ruby is the scripting language. The result is Ruby on Rails, commonly known as Rails or ROR. You can download and install Ruby from *www .ruby-lang.org/en/downloads/*.

Python

```
#!/usr/bin/python
# print statement
print "Hello Cloud"
exit
```

You would save this code in a file named hellocloud.py and then either invoke it by using the command

```
python hellocloud.py
```

or make it an executable file and enter the following command.

```
./hellocloud.py
```

cURL

If you have cURL installed, you can embed cURL commands in PHP scripts. Using cURL makes it easy to do GET/POST requests and receive responses from JSON files. cURL is available in the bash shell and supports various protocols, including FTP, FTPS, HTTP, HTTPS, IMAP, IMAPS, LDAP, LDAPS, SMTP, SMTPS, SCP,

DICT, TFTP, Gopher, and Telnet. The following command downloads "The NIST Definition of Cloud Computing" from the NIST website and stores it on your local driver as nist.pdf.

```
# download a file and store output
curl http://csrc.nist.gov/publications/nistpubs/800-145/SP800-145.pdf >
nist.pdf
```

You can download and install cURL from *www.windows7download.com/win7-curl/download-tjoxvcrw.html*.

Jython

```
#!/usr/bin/jython
# print statement
print "Hello Cloud"
exit
```

Jython is an alternative implementation of Python that is written entirely in Java®. The wsadmin tool uses Jython V2.1 and later. Download and install Jython from *www.jython.org/archive/22/installation.html*.

Node.js

```
console.log("Hello Cloud");
```

You would save the above Node.js script in a JavaScript file named hellocloud.js. If you have Node.js installed, you can run the script using the command

```
node hellocloud.js.
```

The real value of Node.js is routing things to HTTP connections. To do that, you would edit the file as shown in the following example:

```
var http = require('http')
http.createServer(function (request, response) {
    response.writeHead(200, {'Content-Type': 'text/plain'});
    response.end('Hello Cloud\n');
}).listen(8080);
console.log('Node.js Server started');
```

Then, when you run the command node hellocloud.js, you should see Node.js Server started in the command window. Now you can open your Web browser and enter the URL *localhost:8080*. The browser should display "Hello Cloud."

A closer look at that Node.js code shows that the first line saves the HTTP module in a variable. The HTTP module is then used to create an HTTP server via the createServer function, which takes an input parameter and returns an object. Finally, the script calls the listen function on the new server object and specifies port 8080. A function built into the above code takes two parameters—request and response, the details of which you can find in any Node.js programming tutorial. To download Node.js, go to *nodejs.org/*.

Wsadmin Scripting

IBM WebSphere Application Server is the middleware of choice on the IBM Pure-Application platform. Most people who have worked with the WebSphere Application Server are familiar with or have heard of wsadmin. Wsadmin is a scripting interface that is run from the command line and used to manage, configure, and help with WebSphere Application Server runtime operations. You can also use wsadmin scripts to control application deployment.

The wsadmin tool can be run in three modes: interactive, inline, and file input. You can specify the language of the script file, the command, or an interactive shell by using the -lang option. The supported scripting languages are Jacl and Jython. Jython is the recommended choice, being more popular because of its Python roots and having more tooling for developers. You typically embed wsadmin script commands in a script file—more often than not, a Jython script file—then execute the file as needed.

Tip: In the WebSphere Integrated Solutions Console, commonly known as the WebSphere administrative console, you can capture syntax by enabling log command assistance **(System administration > Console Preferences > Log command assistance commands)**. You can then use the commands in scripts.

Wsadmin scripts are most commonly used

- to install JDBC drivers and configure data sources, especially when the database is on-premises;

- to configure Java Message Service resources associated with Service Integration Bus (SIBus) or MQ queue managers;

- for application cluster–specific tasks (e.g., start/stop cluster, node agents); and

- to install apps (e.g., Java Archive, Web Archive, Enterprise Archive, and Broker Archive files).

Listing 4.1 shows an example of a wsadmin command that invokes a Jython script named createDB2Datasource.jy and passes arguments via environment variables prefixed by a dollar sign ($).

```
$WAS_PROFILE_ROOT/bin/wsadmin.sh -lang jython -f

/tmp/createDB2DataSource/createDB2DataSource.jy $CELL_NAME $NODE_NAME

$DATASOURCE_NAME $DATASOURCE_JNDI_NAME $DATABASE_NAME

DATABASE_USERNAME $DATABASE_PASSWORD $DATABASE_HOST $DATABASE_PORT
```

Listing 4.1: Sample wsadmin *command*

Script Packages in PureApplication System

Let's look at how scripts are packaged and loaded onto the IBM PureApplication System. You'll recall that parts, add-ons, and scripts are the building blocks of virtual system patterns, which in turn are one of the types of software pattern that can be deployed on PureApplication. To use a script on PureApplication, you need to zip the file and upload it to the PureApplication catalog.

Script packages by definition are containers that contain all the required components necessary to run a script. The script package itself is a directory compressed into a single file that is uploaded to the catalog and then associated with virtual system patterns. The code included in the script package can be simple or as complex as installing a complete product, such as Splunk or Wily.

At a minimum, your script package should contain a cbscript.json file that references a script file. Most script developers will package three files, as shown in Figure 4.1: a script file, a cbscript.json file, and an extendedattributes.json file, which is optional. These files will be part of the zip file that you upload to the Pure-Application catalog via the console user interface or the command-line interface (CLI). Add-ons and scripts are the two kinds of script packages associated with PureApplication.

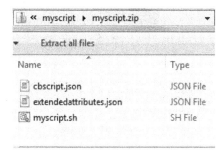

Name	Type
cbscript.json	JSON File
extendedattributes.json	JSON File
myscript.sh	SH File

Figure 4.1: Contents of a simple script package

Tip: If you're developing on a Windows platform, remember to run dos2unix on the script source files before zipping and creating the deployable script package.

Figure 4.2 shows a more real-world example, where the shell script, configure JVMProperties.sh, uses functions defined in traceFunctions.sh and uses wsadmin to invoke configureJVMProperties.py. The configureJVMProperties.py script in turn uses methods that are defined in utils.py and Trace.py. All the configuration parameters are contained in the JVMSettings.properties file.

Name	Size	Packed	Type
..			File folder
utils.py	20,987	4,796	PY File
traceFunctions.sh	3,432	1,399	SH File
Trace.py	56,241	15,183	PY File
JVMSettings.properties	2,561	1,143	PROPERTIES File
configureJVMProperties.sh	14,001	4,783	SH File
configureJVMProperties.py	4,457	1,679	PY File
cbscript.json	537	236	JSON File

ConfigureJVMProperties.zip - ZIP archive, unpacked size 102,216 bytes

Figure 4.2: Contents of a complex script package

When more than a few parameters must be provided for a given script package, you'll probably want to provide those parameters in a properties file, which can be packaged with the script during initial testing. However, the ultimate source of the properties file needs to be a staging server that supports Secure Shell (SSH) or an HTTP server. Later, when the script runs, the properties file can be obtained using SCP, WGET, or cURL. The use of traceFunctions.sh and Trace.py highlights the importance of both UNIX shell and Jython scripts emitting a consistent trace to a log file in order to provide progress and diagnostic information for problem determination.

Tip: A recommended practice is to store the properties file on a staging server that permits read access or supports an HTTP server. The script package should have sufficient information to get the properties file with credentials. SCP, WGET, or cURL can be used to transfer the properties file at runtime to the local directory on the VM on which the script package is being executed.

Uploading a Script Package in PureApplication System

The PureApplication System is preloaded with some default script packages. It also allows developers and system administrators to upload custom script packages via the console user interface. Choose the **Catalog** menu option, then select **Script Packages**; Figure 4.3 shows the interface in the older version of PureApplication; Figure 4.4 shows the V2.1 interface.

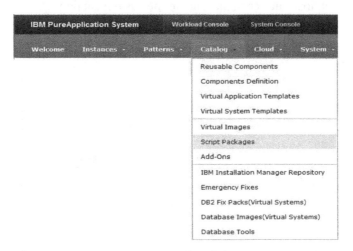

Figure 4.3: Script Packages menu in the PureApplication V1 workload console

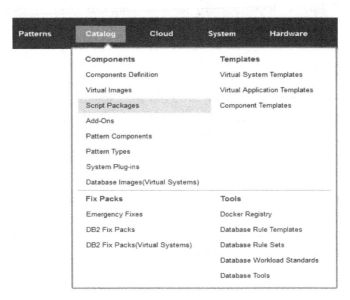

Figure 4.4: Script Packages interface in PureApplication V2.1

The Script Packages screen lists all scripts that are available on the system. You can also click the **Create New** button on the screen to bring up the Import Script Package screen in Figure 4.5. You then browse for the .zip, .tgz, or .tar.gz file and click **Import** to upload the script package to the system catalog.

Figure 4.5: Import Script Package screen

 Tip: Scripts are run on the deployed VM using the root user context. If you want to use a different user context, remember to switch user (su) within the script.

If you plan to develop scripts, there is a file you should know about. It contains all environment variables that are available with the system and provided through the virtual image. After deployment, these variables are located in the virtualimage .properties file on each VM. On Linux and AIX®, the file is located in /etc/virtual image.properties.

The virtualimage.properties file is generated when the VM is deployed based on built-in variables defined in the cbscript.json file and the PureApplication console settings. Each script package can also control what script package variables are stored in virtualimage.properties by using attributes defined in extendedattributes.json. If you view a deployed VM instance in PureApplication's workload console, then go to the virtual machines section and expand the VM, you'll see the option **Show all environment variables**. In Chapter 3 we deployed the IBM BPM Process Server Virtual System Classic Pattern; Figure 4.6 shows a screenshot of the environment variables from the BPMPSDMGR VM that were generated by that deployment.

ADMIN_CONSOLE_URL	https://pas01-grp036.aimsrv.net:9043/ibm/console
APP_SERVICE_COMMAND	/opt/ibm/ae/AS/installAppService.sh
APP_SERVICE_COMMAND_LOG	/opt/IBM/BPM/v85/servicelogs/logs
APP_SERVICE_PACKAGE_LOCATION	/tmp/update/app
DELETE_VIRTUAL_MACHINE	/opt/IBM/BPM/cloud/system/ConfigBPM_Remove_VM.sh
HOSTNAME	pas01-grp036.aimsrv.net
OPERATION_COMMAND_LOCATION	/opt/ibm/ae/AS
OS_NAME	Linux
OS_SERVICE_COMMAND	/opt/ibm/ae/AS/installOSService.sh
OS_SERVICE_COMMAND_LOG	/opt/IBM/BPM/v85/servicelogs/logs
OS_SERVICE_LEVEL	
OS_SERVICE_PACKAGE_LOCATION	/tmp/update/os
OS_TYPE	RedHat Linux
OS_VERSION_LEVEL	2.6.32-358.23.2.el6.x86_64
PART_TYPE_IDENTIFIER	dmgr.procsvr.adv
RESET_VIRTUAL_IMAGE_COMMAND	/var/adm/ibmvmcoc-postinstall/resetvm.sh
RESET_VIRTUAL_IMAGE_COMMAND_LOCATION	/var/adm/ibmvmcoc-postinstall
SERVICE_COMMAND	/opt/ibm/ae/AS/installService.sh
SERVICE_COMMAND_LOCATION	/opt/ibm/ae/AS
SERVICE_COMMAND_LOG	/opt/IBM/BPM/v85/servicelogs
SERVICE_PACKAGE_LOCATION	/tmp/update
START_SERVICES_COMMAND	/opt/ibm/ae/AS/startVirtualImageServices.sh
START_SERVICES_COMMAND_LOCATION	/opt/ibm/ae/AS
STOP_SERVICES_COMMAND	/opt/ibm/ae/AS/stopVirtualImageServices.sh
STOP_SERVICES_COMMAND_LOCATION	/opt/ibm/ae/AS
VNC_SERVER_URL	http://pas01-grp036.aimsrv.net:5801/
WAS_CONTROL_HOME	/opt/ibm/ae/AS

Figure 4.6: Environment variables from the BPMPSDMGR *VM*

Basic Scripting

Script packages can include any set of executable files and components, from a UNIX shell script (.sh), to one or more Python files (.py), to cURL commands. This section lists a few basic scripts.

A Simple Python Script

Using your favorite text editor, enter the code in Listing 4.2 into a file and name it import.py. This sample script uses Python 2.7 and demonstrates how to import modules—in this case, the sys and string modules.

```
import <module_name>
#
# import.py
#
import sys
import string
#
# sys.platform shows you what OS you are operating on.
# sys.version shows the version of Python.
#
print sys.platform
print sys.version
#
# create a variable called firstspace and give it the value
# of that portion of the string returned by sys.version
# up to the first space.
#
firstspace = string.find(sys.version, ' ')
#
# create another variable called ver and give it the value
# of firstspace.
```

Continued

Listing 4.2: Import.py script

```
#                                                        Listing 4.2 Continued

ver = sys.version[:firstspace]


print 'I am running on %s platform.' % sys.platform

print 'I am running PYTHON version %s on a %s platform.' % (ver,
sys.platform

dummy = raw_input()
```

 Tip: A Python script can run on any operating system.

A Simple UNIX Shell Script

Using your favorite text editor, type the code shown in Listing 4.3 into a file, and name the file echoArgs.sh. This shell script echoes the two command-line arguments: user and password. It shows the syntax for passing values from the command line to a script and, as most scripts do, it checks whether the Java environment is set up.

```
#!/bin/bash

#

# FILE          : echoArgs.sh

# DESCRIPTION   : The script takes 2 arguments

#                 LOGINUSER              user

#                 LOGINPASSWORD          password

#
                                                                Continued
```

Listing 4.3: Echoargs.sh *script*

Listing 4.3 continued

```
umask 022

if [ $# -ne 2 ]; then
  echo "ERROR: Invalid number of arguments"
  echo "Usage: $0 <LOGINUSER> <LOGINPASSWORD>"
  echo "e.g. $0 was61 Secret123"
  exit 1
fi


LOGINUSER=${1}
LOGINPASSWORD=${2}


# check environment
if [ -z ${JAVA_HOME} ]; then
  echo "ERROR: Environment variable JAVA_HOME not defined."
  echo "Set JAVA_HOME and re-run this script."
  exit 1
fi


USERROOT='dirname ${CONFIG_ROOT}'
BINDIR=${USERROOT}/bin
PROPDIR=${USERROOT}/properties
TEMPDIR=${USERROOT}/temp


DATESTAMP='date -u +"%Y%m%d"'


echo
```

Continued

```
echo "${0} completed successfully"                          Listing 4.3 continued

echo
```

When developing complex scripts, you should log messages frequently. Quite often, logged messages provide the only means of tracing execution in the event of an error.

Anatomy of cbscript.json

The cbscript.json object describes the script package and points to the location of the main executable. It can also contain all the configuration parameters, which allows the configuration definition to remain consistent whenever the script package is used. No matter which scripting language you choose, your scripts will always be packaged with a cbscript.json object.

The code in Listing 4.4 shows the special JSON object that includes information about the packaged script. The code snippet is from a script package to start WebSphere Application Server (WAS) clusters. This particular cbscript.json object has command arguments (commandargs) but no optional arguments—that is, no key/value pairs. Notice the beginning and ending square brackets in the file.

The commandargs arguments are an optional list of arguments whose values are passed to the script at runtime. When the script package is uploaded to the catalog, the list of arguments is displayed in the Arguments field of the Script Packages pane. The string can have a maximum of 4,098 characters and can include environment variables.

```
[
{
    "version": "1.0.0",

    "description": "This script package starts clusters",

    "command": "${WAS_PROFILE_ROOT}/bin/wsadmin.sh",

    "log": "${WAS_PROFILE_ROOT}/logs/",                        Continued
```

Listing 4.4: Sample cbscript.json object

```
    "location": "/tmp/scripts",                    Listing 4.4 continued

    "timeout": "0",

    "commandargs": "-conntype JSR160RMI -port 9809 -user ${WAS_USERNAME}
-password ${WAS_PASSWORD} -lang jython -f /tmp/scripts/
start-clusters.py all"

}

]
```

Variables within the script can use the following syntax to access the values passed by the command-line arguments:

```
var = sys.argv[index]
```

Listing 4.5 shows the corresponding script file that uses wsadmin commands to start the two WebSphere Application Server clusters—HVMsgCluster and HVWebCluster.

```
AdminControl.invoke('WebSphere:name=HVMsgCluster_1,process=dmgr,platform=
common,node=CloudBurstNode_1,version=8.0.0.4,type=Cluster,mbeanIdentifier=
HVMsgCluster_1,cell=CloudBurstCell_1,spec=1.0', 'start')

AdminControl.invoke('WebSphere:name=HVWebCluster_1,process=dmgr,platform=
common,node=CloudBurstNode_1,version=8.0.0.4,type=Cluster,mbeanIdentifier=
HVWebCluster_1,cell=CloudBurstCell_1,spec=1.0', 'start')
```

Listing 4.5: Script to start WAS clusters

Tip: Do not use the default timeout value of 0, because it basically indicates no timeout. Always have a timeout value of 180000 or so (the unit is milliseconds) to allow time to recover from script errors and enable debugging.

Listing 4.6 shows a cbscript.json file that has environment variables denoted as keys. Keys are a list of environment variables that are added to other system environment variables made available to the script at runtime. When the script package is uploaded to the system catalog, these environment variables and their values are displayed in the Environment field of the Script Packages pane.

```json
{

    "name": "Install SSFS silently",

    "version": "1.0.0",

    "description": "This script package installs SSFS 9.2 silently",

    "command": "/bin/sh /tmp/installSSFS/installSSFS.sh",

    "log": "/tmp/installSSFS",

    "location": "/tmp/installSSFS",

    "timeout": "0",

    "commandargs": "",

    "keys":

    [

        {

          "scriptkey": "SSFS_JAR_FILE",

          "scriptvalue": "",

          "scriptdefaultvalue": "SMCFS_9.2.0.jar"

        },

        {

          "scriptkey": "FTP_SERVER",

          "scriptvalue": "",

          "scriptdefaultvalue": "172.16.72.31"

        },

        {
```

Continued

Listing 4.6: Sample cbscript.json with keys

```
        "scriptkey": "FTP_USER",                    Listing 4.6 continued

        "scriptvalue": "",

        "scriptdefaultvalue": "anonymous"

      },

      {

        "scriptkey": "FTP_PASSWORD",

        "scriptvalue": "",

        "scriptdefaultvalue": "my@company.com"

      }

    ]

}
```

You'll notice that the command line is set to execute a shell script package named installSSFS.sh. The keys that are passed as environment variables are SSFS_JAR_FILE, FTP_SERVER, FTP_USER, and FTP_PASSWORD. Each key or environment variable is defined by three values: scriptkey, scriptvalue, and scriptdefaultvalue.

As mentioned earlier, all the environment variables (key/value pairs) will be appended to the /etc/virtualimages.properties file during the deployment of the pattern or creation of the VM. Listing 4.7 shows the first iteration of the corresponding script, named installSSFS.sh.

```
#!/bin/sh

#*****************************************************************

#

#   Source File Name: installSSFS.sh

#

#   Function:

                                                        Continued
```

Listing 4.7: Sample shell script InstallSSFS.sh

```
#    Copy SSFS Jar and response file to /tmp for installation

#

#  Operating System: Linux

#

#  Authors: IBM

#

#*********************************************************************


echo "DB2INSTANCE=db2inst1" >> /etc/virtualimage.properties


echo "FTP_SERVER="$FTP_SERVER >> /tmp/installSSFS/installSSFS.log

echo "FTP_USER="$FTP_USER >> /tmp/installSSFS/installSSFS.log

echo "FTP_PASSWORD="$FTP_PASSWORD >> /tmp/installSSFS/installSSFS.log

echo "SSFS_JAR_FILE="$SSFS_JAR_FILE >> /tmp/installSSFS/installSSFS.log

echo "DB_HOST="$DB_HOST >> /tmp/installSSFS/installSSFS.log


export LANG=en_US

export LC_ALL=en_US

echo "LANG="$LANG >> /tmp/installSSFS/installSSFS.log

chmod 777 -R /opt/IBM/WebSphere/SSFS

ls -l /opt/IBM/WebSphere >> /tmp/installSSFS/installSSFS.log


echo "Unzip JARs" >> /tmp/installSSFS/installSSFS.log


# unzip /tmp/installSSFS/SMCFS_9.2.0.zip

unzip -d $WAS_INSTALL_ROOT/java/lib /tmp/installSSFS/endorsed.zip
```

Continued

81

Listing 4.7 continued

```
echo "FTP SSFS jar file" >> /tmp/installSSFS/installSSFS.log

curl -u $FTP_USER:$FTP_PASSWORD -o /tmp/installSSFS/$SSFS_JAR_FILE
ftp://$FTP_SERVER/$SSFS_JAR_FILE


echo "DB_HOST="$DB_HOST >> /tmp/installSSFS/silentSSFS.txt


# silently install SSFS

echo "Install SSFS" >> /tmp/installSSFS/installSSFS.log

su - virtuser -c "cd /opt/IBM/WebSphere/SSFS; export LANG=en_US;
$WAS_INSTALL_ROOT/java/bin/java -jar /tmp/installSSFS/$SSFS_JAR_FILE
-f /tmp/installSSFS/silentSSFS.txt"
```

There are times when you may not want script package variables ending up in virtualimage.properties, and you may want those variables to be visible only to the script package in which they are defined. The properties that control whether the script package variables are added to virtualimage.properties and whether they are visible outside the script package are savevars and envonly, respectively. These properties are part of extendedattributes.json, which as mentioned earlier is an optional file in a script package. Savevars and envonly are the options available to you when you add extendedattributes.json to a script package.

All the automation and ease that cloud computing brings can be attributed to scripting. It is a critical part of making things work in the cloud, and one that is usually hidden from the end users. But those who are responsible for setting up and implementing cloud solutions have no choice but to get their hands dirty with writing scripts.

Recommended Practices

Applying scripts to cloud development can make short work of deploying patterns and other cloud-related tasks. Here are some recommended practices that experienced script developers follow:

- Set up a naming convention before you write your first script and make sure all developers on the project adhere to it.

- Whenever possible, create scripts on their target platform to avoid unanticipated problems. For example, there are slight differences between how scripts run on a Linux platform and how they run on an AIX platform.

- Use fully qualified configuration parameter names; the notation is PART_NAME.property. For example ${DMGRPart.ipaddr} is used to retrieve the DMgr IP address from a script in any part of the virtual system.

- Mount NFS to upload large binaries. Using NFS reduces the script package size and the time it takes to upload the package.

- Remember to test connectivity to an FTP server so binaries can be downloaded to it.

- Get into the habit of continuous testing: develop, deploy, test, repeat.

- Use trace to log files and stdout to log every major step that's completed and to log error conditions and exception stacks in all scripts.

PureApplication System Command-Line Interface

All cloud platforms have a CLI for running native commands. The CLI can be executed from any desktop or laptop. The interface for PureApplication System provides a scripting environment based on Jython. You can either embed commands into scripts or download the CLI and use it in interactive mode.

With PureApplication, you can download the CLI to any desktop computer and then point to the host system in order to communicate with it. Thus, you can manage the platform remotely. To download the PureApplication CLI, click the **Download Tooling** link from the Welcome page of either the workload console or the system console, then select **Download command line tool**, as shown in Figure 4.7.

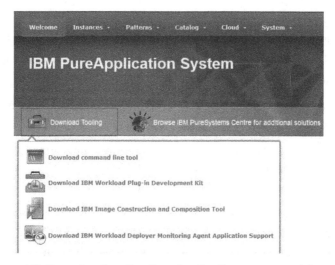

Figure 4.7: Downloading the PureApplication command-line tool

Save the zip file, then extract the contents to a folder on your workstation. Extracting the zip file creates a directory named pure.cli that contains four subfolders: bin, lib, logs, and samples. The directory also contains a README.txt file. If you navigate to the samples folder, you'll see the various built-in Python and Jython scripts, as shown in Figure 4.8. Script developers can extend or customize these scripts for use in custom script packages. The sample scripts that are especially worth noting are deployPattern.py, exportPattern.py, and importPatterns.py.

 Tip: In PureApplication V2.1, the unzipped contents of the CLI display a new folder named Docker.

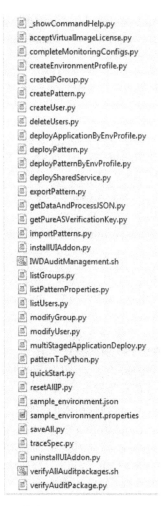

Figure 4.8: Contents of the samples folder

If you navigate to the pure.cli/ bin directory, you can find the executable (which is named pure.bat on Windows systems) used to run Jython scripts from the command line. The syntax for the pure command is

```
pure.bat -h <PureApp_HOST_NAME> -u <USER_NAME> -p <PASSWORD> -a -f
jython-script.py
```

For example, the following command, executed from the folder to which the CLI was unzipped, deploys a pattern from the command line after connecting to the host specified by the IP address:

```
pure.bat -h 19.86.114.33 -u admin -p password -a -f ..\samples\
deployPattern.py
```

Add-Ons

Add-ons are specialized scripts that let you customize the hardware and operating system of VMs. At deployment time, all add-on operations are executed before the custom script packages are run. A set of default add-ons is provided with the initial configuration of PureApplication System. You can use these as is, clone and modify them as needed, or create new ones and add them to the catalog.

In the PureApplication user interface, go to the workload console and click **Catalog > Add-Ons** to view the list of available add-ons, which include scripts for tasks such as adding a raw disk, adding a virtual interface controller (NIC), and defining an extra user on a VM.

Using the Plug-in Development Kit

You can, of course, create script packages and other PureApplication-related components by using your favorite editor. However, if you want to create new add-ons, we recommend using the Plug-in Development Kit, also known as the PDK. You can download the PDK from PureApplication's workload console Welcome screen. The user interface has been rearranged a bit in the latest version of PureApplication, as shown in Figure 4.9. Now both the CLI and the PDK are available from the **Download Tooling** option in the PureApplication console.

Figure 4.9: PureApplication's Download Tooling option in V2

You need to have the Apache Ant® utility installed on your workstation; it's available at *ant.apache.org*. After downloading the PDK, unzip it to a folder (for example, C:\IPAS\pdk1.1) and then run Ant. Look for the BUILD SUCCESSFUL message. If you list the contents of that folder now, you should see a zip file named com.ibm.maestro.plugin.pdk.site.zip. You'll need to import this file into your Eclipse framework.

To bring up your Eclipse framework and install new software, go to **Help > Install New Software > Add > Archive**. Browse to the zip file com.ibm.maestro .plugin.pdk.site.zip, then give it a name, as in Figure 4.10, and click **OK**.

Figure 4.10: Adding the PDK repository location in Eclipse

On the Available Software screen, make sure you select **Contact all update sites during install to find required software** and continue with the prompts to install the PDK. When you're finished, restart Eclipse, and the Welcome screen shown in Figure 4.11 (see page 88) will be displayed.

Now you're almost ready to start developing patterns and scripts for Pure-Application System. You can get to the workspace by clicking the curved arrow. To return to the welcome screen at any time, simply go to the Help menu and choose the Welcome option.

Before you start developing a plug-in, verify that Eclipse can communicate with the PureApplication System. In the main menu, go to **Window > Preferences** and highlight **IBM Plug-in Toolkit**. Enter the fully qualified host name or IP address of the PureApplication system, a user ID, and a password, then click **Test Connection**. When the connection is successful, you'll see a window similar to that shown in Figure 4.12. Click **OK** and proceed with developing your plug-in.

Figure 4.11: Plug-in Development Kit in Eclipse framework

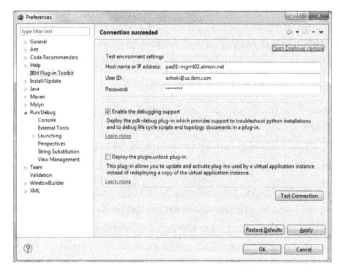

Figure 4.12: PureApplication System connection screen for the Plug-in Toolkit

When you are ready to create a pattern project or a script project, use the Workload Pattern Development perspective. To open this perspective, click **Window > Open Perspective > Other > Workload Pattern Development**. On the main canvas, the Welcome page should display the PDK User Guide, as in Figure 4.13. Simply click one of the Create Project links to start.

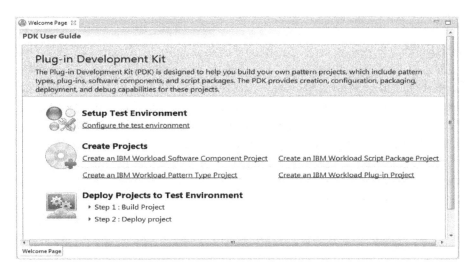

Figure 4.13: Plug-in Development Kit welcome screen

Tip: Look for Workload Pattern and Workload Runtime perspectives under **Window > Open Perspective > Other**.

One important feature of using the PDK is that you can directly deploy your project to a VM instance running on PureApplication System. When you're ready to deploy a project, you should use the runtime perspective. To bring up the runtime perspective, click **Window > Open Perspective > Other > Workload Plug-in**

Runtime. The runtime perspective lets you manage test deployments by directly connecting to a running VM on the PureApplication system. All you have to do is open a connection and specify the VM's IP address.

Script packages might be simple enough to be created manually in a text editor. But if you're attempting to create a new software component for use in PureApplication System V2.*x*, you really should use the PDK.

Cloudlets

Even in the world of converged systems and patterns of expertise, developers have to be ready to roll up their sleeves and start coding. Cloud platform vendors have come a long way in providing most of the default configuration and various building blocks, but there is still the need to develop custom code, test it, and deploy it. That development and test cycle has been accelerated and has given rise to what is commonly known in cloud environments as DevOps. And most cloud platforms provide the associated tools or frameworks to help developers and administrators create the required components.

5

Services Layers and Services in the Cloud

A key distinction between Infrastructure as a Service (IaaS) and Platform as a Service (PaaS) is the type of service offered by each segment. With IaaS, consumers usually work with virtualized servers that they can configure themselves, whereas with PaaS, the consumer uses and works with services that are created and maintained by the cloud service provider. Figure 5.1 captures the basic differences between IaaS and PaaS.

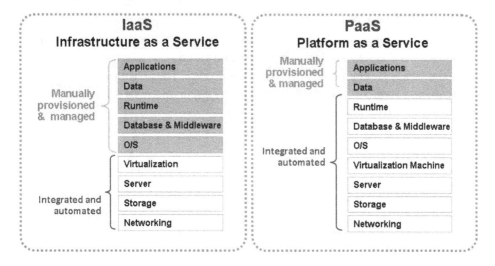

Figure 5.1: Difference between IaaS and PaaS

When PaaS is discussed, it is often construed to be in the private cloud domain. But in fact these services are increasingly available on public clouds. Is there a difference between services available in a private cloud and those available in a public cloud? From a cloud service consumer perspective it shouldn't matter, although if the consumer is an enterprise client, questions of security and workload isolation come up. But from the cloud service provider perspective, many things need to be addressed.

Recently we've been hearing a lot about public PaaS platforms such as Heroku, Bluemix, and Azure. They all run on some infrastructure, the services for which are provided by hosting providers such as Rackspace®, SoftLayer, and Amazon Web Services®. This chapter touches upon IaaS, using IBM's SoftLayer to explain the concepts. References to other products illustrate the fact that there is quite a bit of commonality between cloud hosting providers.

Characteristics of a Public Cloud

In its broadest definition, a public cloud is a set of computing resources set up based upon a cloud computing model in which a service provider makes IT resources publicly available over the Internet. There are basically three types of resources—compute, storage, and network—which may be offered free on a trial basis, for a fixed monthly fee, or on a pay-as-you-go model. IaaS providers host hardware, middleware, servers, storage, and other infrastructure components for their users. IaaS providers can also host users' applications and handle tasks such as system maintenance and backup. In addition to the three cloud service models, NIST has defined four deployment models, shown in Figure 5.2. These deployment models are classified according to where the service is running and what kind of access is provided.

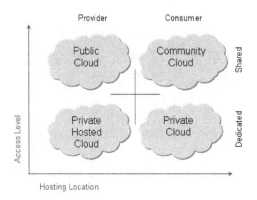

Figure 5.2: Cloud deployment models

Enterprises have security concerns, which I discuss in a later section. Notwithstanding those concerns, the many benefits to public cloud computing include:

- All resources are readily available for clients to start quick deployments.

- Clients pay only for resources that are consumed.

- Resources can be rapidly scaled based on need.

- All services are delivered in a consistent manner.

Figure 5.3 shows a cloud network topology. It depicts the cloud environment as accessible from the Internet over a public or external network. The routing switch, or cloud gateway, uses the internal network to communicate with cloud resources. These resources, which can be VMs or bare-metal servers, are accessible via various ports within the cloud. If one were to add more details to this figure, one could show the cloud load balancers, which route traffic to different instances in the cloud; caching instances; database instances; and other cloud block storage components.

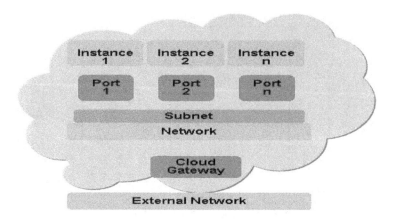

Figure 5.3: Public cloud network topology

Cloud service models are also defined by the ownership and degree of customization allowed, which translate into cost, control, and elasticity. Those metrics determine whether the cloud services are fully managed or unmanaged and how much can be done in-house versus what can be outsourced.

Managed vs. Unmanaged Services

Cloud services typically come in one of two forms: managed and unmanaged. Managed services offer support for every task and problem related to the resources hosted by the provider. With unmanaged services, the provider will replace failed hardware components, but does not support software installations or patch upgrades. Some cloud providers offer both managed services and unmanaged services, including support for backup and restore services.

An enterprise's in-house expertise, consumption appetite, and costs will dictate which option it chooses. While some clients choose unmanaged servers, apply their own security configuration, and use the servers for rapidly deploying development and test environments, others may have a fully managed infrastructure for rolling out their production topology. Table 5.1 lists some of the features of both managed and unmanaged services.

Table 5.1: Managed versus unmanaged cloud services

Managed Services	Unmanaged Services
Operating system deployment and management	Operating system deployment
Client is given controlled access to operating system	Client is given complete control over operating system
Monitoring and notification	Unrestricted access to servers and any software the client needs installed
Maintenance and routine patching	Initially cheaper to sign up because there is no management or maintenance support
Backup and restore services	Client is responsible for backing up components
Disaster recovery and storage services	Client is responsible for storage and recovery
Security services	Client is responsible for installing security patches
OS-based service-level agreements	Hypervisor-only or infrastructure-only service-level agreements

Unmanaged servers are less expensive and give you greater freedom to control your servers, whereas managed servers mandate the use of certain processes and tools for control. With unmanaged servers, one also inherits the risks of misconfigurations and the responsibility of dealing with application failures. Managed cloud services usually come with a more long-term agreement between the cloud service consumer and the cloud service provider. So, while both types of services have their advantages and disadvantages, the key is to understand your own organization's skill set and needs and choose appropriately.

Note: As a common practice, enterprises tend to opt for managed services for their production environments and choose unmanaged services for non-production environments.

Workload Isolation and Security

Workload isolation involves placing workloads in the cloud such that the resources they use do not adversely affect other applications running in the same cloud. In contrast, security deals with keeping applications, especially the data, private and secure from other applications in the cloud.

In addition to providing workload security, cloud service providers are often faced with demonstrating workload isolation. While workloads might share common pools of resources under normal circumstances, they need to be isolated from each other so that problems in one workload do not affect other workloads. Similarly, sensitive data in one workload should not be visible in any shape or form to other workloads. Isolated workloads each get their own set of dedicated resources.

Other levels of isolation include network isolation, isolation of management networks, data network isolation, and isolation of IP storage networks. Isolation can be physical or logical. Physical segmentation of networks, allowing only authorized administrators access to networks, and using non-routable networks are some of the ways of keeping each client's environment separate from other clients' environments. While cloud service providers strive to provide these various levels of isolation, the inherent isolation provided by cloud containers is one of the main reasons that the use of container technology is increasing. (More about containers later in this chapter.)

 Note: Physical isolation means the resources are running on separate hardware. Logical isolation uses hardware-management software to make a single set of hardware work like multiple, separate sets of hardware.

In a private cloud platform such as the PureApplication System, workload isolation is facilitated through cloud groups and smart placement algorithms. You'll recall from Chapter 2 that cloud groups contain compute nodes and a reference locator, such as an IP group. Thus a cloud group has all the components needed to run VMs, as shown in Figure 5.4.

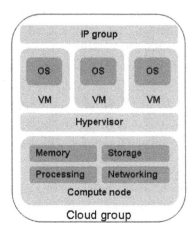

Figure 5.4: A cloud group in PureApplication System

Placement of the VM instance is crucial to achieving workload isolation. When placing a new VM instance, the placement algorithm in PureApplication System selects the compute node based on effective capacity. Resources such as CPU, memory, data network bandwidth, and storage network bandwidth are used in the placement calculation. For more information about workload isolation in PureApplication System, see *www.ibm.com/developerworks/cloud/library/cl-ps-aim1302-workisolation/*.

In the public cloud, workload isolation is provided by the underlying cloud infrastructure. Along with placement constraints, a combination of networking and security technologies is used to isolate traffic.

You've likely heard it said that you should not trust a cloud service provider to protect your corporate assets. Indeed, security has become the most common inhibitor for enterprises that would like to adopt cloud computing, and rightfully so. Two facets of security—threats and compliance—dictate access controls. On one hand, enterprises are forced to address a growing number of mandates, including national regulations, local mandates, and industry standards. On the other hand, enterprises have to shield themselves from threats both external and internal. Enterprises must be constantly vigilant against threats ranging from cyberattacks and corporate espionage to disgruntled employee actions and internal careless breaches.

Even though many of the security concerns are not new, to gain the trust of organizations, cloud service providers must meet or exceed the security and privacy that's available in traditional IT. Additionally, sensitive data such as credit card information stored on-premises should always be encrypted. Some cloud service providers offer encryption services within their cloud-based storage. Many third-party security products, such as CipherCloud® and SecureCloud™, monitor the data that's stored in the cloud and prevent malicious data from penetrating the client's system. A website being hosted in the cloud can use website protection services.

Once cloud security requirements are understood, we can use the Cloud Computing Reference Architecture with foundational security controls when designing, deploying, and consuming cloud services. The controls around security are

- cloud governance
- risk management and compliance
- security incident management
- identity and access management
- discovery, categorization, and protection of data and information assets
- virtual systems acquisition, development, and maintenance
- management of threats and vulnerabilities
- physical and personnel security

The need for privacy and security is why many enterprises start with a private or on-premises cloud that has such security controls. Once an enterprise has processes in place to protect virtualized environments from outside attacks, it can move into hybrid and public cloud solutions.

Virtualization is fundamental to cloud computing. But the proliferation of virtual images raises the risk of malicious attacks and exploitation of security flaws. Remember, the hypervisor is the traffic cop that controls multiple images of various resources. The hypervisor relies on the underlying operating system to manage and protect the applications and interfaces. It all boils down to protecting the integrity of customer data and ensuring a good customer experience. End users and customers are mainly concerned about the quality of service within a secure environment.

Note: From data breaches to shared technology vulnerabilities, the Cloud Security Alliance's Top Threats Working Group has identified the top nine cloud computing threats, which it calls The Notorious Nine. You can download the report at *cloudsecurityalliance.org/download/ the-notorious-nine-cloud-computing-top-threats-in-2013/*.

Overview of SoftLayer

SoftLayer, an IBM company, is a cloud service provider that specializes in the self-service model. Customers wanting to move their workloads to the cloud can go to *www.softlayer.com*, specify the resources they want, and get access to their portion of the cloud in a matter of hours.

Like Rackspace and Amazon Web Services, SoftLayer offers cloud computing infrastructure as a service—IaaS. In other words, SoftLayer is a dedicated-server, managed-hosting, and cloud-computing provider. It has a global presence, and its cloud infrastructure is optimized for born-on-the-cloud applications at Internet scale. The infrastructure provided by SoftLayer can be bare-metal servers or virtualized servers, unmanaged or managed, and deployed using a public, private, or hybrid cloud model. Users get a single-pane portal to control and tune all services.

SoftLayer is available globally and seamlessly across national borders. That ubiquity is possible because SoftLayer's data centers are connected by an advanced network that integrates distinct public, private, and internal management networks offering better access than other cloud providers and high speeds that reach 2 TB per second between locations.

Since SoftLayer, like Rackspace and Amazon Web Services, follows a self-service model, all you need to do is go to the SoftLayer website and choose the resource or resources you want under PRODUCTS & SERVICES at the top of the page. As Figure 5.5 shows, you can choose from basic three resources—servers, storage, and networking—and specify how you want the services customized based on your security, development, and management needs.

Figure 5.5: SoftLayer's self-service portal

To continue, you need to know what to order and how much of a particular resource you need. Every bit carries an additional cost. For example, choosing Virtual Servers brings up the sliding gauge shown in Figure 5.6. As you increase the cores and RAM, the hourly and monthly costs rise.

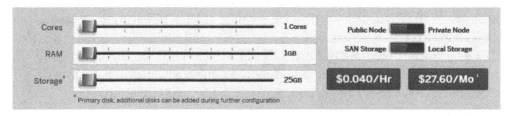

Figure 5.6: Choosing virtual servers from SoftLayer

Rackspace (*www.rackspace.com*) is similar: You need to know what to order and how much of it, as in Figure 5.7. The beauty of such self-service systems and the cloud infrastructure in general is that you can change your requirements at any time. The pricing is typically a combination of infrastructure and the chosen service level. If you have the expertise, you can opt for basic managed infrastructure. On the other end of the spectrum, if you want the provider to manage the entire cloud operation for you, including monitoring, maintenance, backup, and patching, you can ask for fully managed operations. SoftLayer, Rackspace, and other cloud platform providers offer every flavor of operating system, virtualization layers, different software languages and frameworks, databases, messaging software, Web servers, and security services.

OS: LINUX | SERVICE LEVEL: MANAGED INFRASTRUCTURE | DISPLAY: HOURLY

Name	RAM	vCPUs[1]	System Disk[2]	Data Disk[3]	Bandwidth[4]	Raw Infrastructure		Managed Infrastructure
General1-1	1GB	1	20GB SSD	—	200Mb/s	$0.032/hr	+	$0.005/hr
General1-2	2GB	2	40GB SSD	—	400Mb/s	$0.064/hr	+	$0.010/hr
General1-4	4GB	4	80GB SSD	—	800Mb/s	$0.128/hr	+	$0.020/hr
General1-8	8GB	8	160GB SSD	—	1,600Mb/s	$0.256/hr	+	$0.040/hr

The Managed Infrastructure service level has a minimum monthly service charge of $50 across all Cloud Servers (virtual and bare metal).

Figure 5.7: Choosing cloud resources from the Rackspace portal

SoftLayer's Looking Glass portal at *lg.softlayer.com* gives you a view of the network routing information and latency times of the backbone infrastructure. Figure 5.8 shows a snapshot of the network latency of the SoftLayer IP Backbone. When you hover over any cell, details of latency and data loss are displayed.

SoftLayer IP Backbone - Network Latency

All | North America | Europe | Asia / Pacific

	ATL	CHI	DAL	DEN	HOU	LAX	MEX	MIA	MON	NYC	SEA	SJC	TOR	WDC	AMS	FRA	LON	PAR	HKG	MEL	SNG	SYD	TOK
ATL	0	32	21	34	28	52	41	13	28	18	60	60	33	13	91	97	90	93	205	200	234	213	151
CHI	32	0	24	26	32	57	43	43	19	22	45	52	11	19	95	104	91	97	197	197	213	212	146
DAL	21	24	0	15	7	32	22	30	44	45	41	36	35	34	111	118	114	117	181	181	215	192	130
DEN	34	26	15	0	23	34	36	44	45	47	27	27	36	44	120	132	115	122	175	184	195	196	122
HOU	28	32	7	23	0	33	26	24	48	46	49	43	40	41	120	126	115	125	177	185	209	202	143
LAX	52	57	32	34	33	0	48	59	67	75	25	8	65	65	139	147	144	147	151	150	173	163	107
MEX	41	43	22	36	26	48	0	50	62	63	62	56	56	54	132	143	135	141	201	197	209	210	155
MIA	13	43	30	44	24	59	50	0	40	30	69	68	46	27	104	112	99	105	204	209	230	221	167
MON	28	19	44	45	48	67	62	40	0	10	64	71	10	15	83	88	79	85	216	216	233	237	176
NYC	18	22	45	47	46	75	63	30	10	0	66	75	15	6	73	78	69	76	225	222	240	230	173
SEA	60	45	41	27	49	25	62	69	64	66	0	18	56	63	140	148	134	139	167	174	185	187	123
SJC	60	52	36	27	43	8	55	68	71	75	18	0	63	71	147	156	141	149	144	157	162	171	100
TOR	33	11	35	36	40	65	56	46	10	15	56	63	0	21	89	96	84	91	200	211	230	227	163
WDC	13	19	34	44	41	65	54	27	15	6	63	71	21	0	80	86	75	82	219	213	243	226	170
AMS	91	95	111	120	120	139	132	104	83	73	140	147	89	80	0	7	6	15	292	294	309	306	241
FRA	97	104	118	132	126	147	143	112	88	78	148	156	96	86	7	0	14	10	296	300	321	310	257
LON	90	91	114	115	115	144	135	99	79	69	134	141	84	75	6	14	0	7	284	292	308	307	241
PAR	93	97	117	122	125	147	141	105	85	76	139	149	91	82	15	10	7	0	291	293	314	313	252
HKG	205	197	181	175	177	151	201	204	216	225	167	144	200	219	292	296	284	291	0	170	33	159	43
MEL	200	197	181	184	185	150	197	209	219	222	174	157	211	213	294	300	292	293	170	0	194	14	127
SNG	234	213	215	195	209	173	209	230	233	240	185	162	230	243	309	321	308	314	33	194	0	181	69
SYD	210	212	195	197	199	163	211	222	237	237	187	171	224	228	302	312	306	309	159	14	181	0	113
TOK	151	146	130	122	143	107	155	167	176	173	123	100	163	170	241	257	241	252	43	127	69	113	0

Figure 5.8: Network latency times from the SoftLayer Looking Glass portal

If you sign up for an account on SoftLayer, you'll receive a URL and credentials to log in and access your servers. That's all there is to accessing the infrastructure in the public cloud.

Monitoring vs. Chargeback

The term *chargeback* refers to charging IT or resource usage to different business units of a company or to billing other companies for resource use. But before you can charge for services, you have to monitor usage. All public cloud providers have free basic monitoring services that customers can use. For example, among the various products and services offered by the SoftLayer interface that was shown in Figure 5.5 is a category called Monitoring & Reporting. The entire infrastructure stack should be continuously monitored to make sure the applications are up and running all the time. Additionally, the cloud service provider should send notifications and provide real-time alerts. If you have a fully managed solution, you can specify what you want to have monitored and how you want to be notified, and the cloud platform provider will take care of the rest.

Obviously there are different levels of monitoring, and their costs vary. Organizations that already have enterprise-level monitoring in their IT department can use monitoring agents on the cloud platform. Figure 5.9 shows the three monitoring levels and various agents available on the SoftLayer platform.

	Basic	Advanced	Premium
Comprehensive infrastructure and services visibility	•	•	•
Full transparency through any application stack	•	•	•
High-levels of security, availability, and scalability	•	•	•
Tiered monitoring levels to meet targeted business objectives and needs	•	•	•
Robust APIs for extensive integration	•	•	•
Lightweight, scalable architecture + "zero-touch" deployment	•	•	•
Network Traffic Monitoring Agent	×	•	•
DHCP Response Monitoring Agent	×	•	•
File and Directory Checking Agent	×	•	•
LDAP Response Monitoring Agent	×	•	•
Mounted File System Monitoring Agent	×	•	•
Network Time Protocol Response Monitoring Agent	×	•	•
Process Monitoring Agent	×	•	•
SNMP Data Monitoring Agent	×	×	•
Performance Monitoring Agent	×	×	•
Apache Monitoring Agent	×	×	•
DNS Response Monitoring Agent	×	×	•
Email Response Monitoring Agent	×	×	•
IIS Monitoring Agent	×	×	•
MSSQL Monitoring Agent	×	×	•
MySQL Monitoring Agent	×	×	•
Tomcat Server Monitoring Agent	×	×	•
URL Response Monitoring Agent	×	×	•

Figure 5.9: Monitoring options from SoftLayer

Amazon CloudWatch is a monitoring service for Amazon Web Services cloud resources and the applications that run on it. Amazon CloudWatch can collect and track metrics, collect and monitor log files, and set alarms or notifications. Details are available at *aws.amazon.com/cloudwatch/*.

Similarly, through what it calls Rackspace Cloud Monitoring, Rackspace offers remote monitoring, agent monitoring, alarms and notifications, and even its own monitoring mobile app. You can find all related information at *www.rackspace.com/ cloud/monitoring/*.

One refrain that has limited cloud adoption within enterprises is that there is a lack of clear chargeback to business units that share the resources. This criticism was true a few years back, especially for private cloud environments. Nowadays, however, there are tools that are available on-premises, or you can use cloud services and even third-party packages to track the use of cloud computing resources.

Building accounting tools in-house is definitely not recommended. So after you choose your accounting tool or technology, you'll have to decide how you want to bill for cloud resources and services. The three most common accounting models are

- "all you can eat"
- according to quantity of resources used
- according to amount of time spent

The "all you can eat" approach is an unsophisticated yet popular options, wherein enterprises set aside a sum of money each month based on the estimated use of cloud computing resources and charge the entire amount to the enterprise budget. The downside to this approach is that a few heavy users of the cloud will make out well because the cost is shared disproportionately by others who may have far less use for such resources.

Billing based on the quantity of resources used is very similar to the data plans for mobile phone billing. Some cloud service providers track how much data is transmitted to and from the cloud and bill the consumer accordingly. But that approach simply measures transmission traffic between the customer and the cloud and does not accurately reflect the internal use of cloud resources. A better way is for consumers to pay for the amount of disk, memory, and CPU they use. Hence many cloud service providers offer tiered services and charge clients based on the tier the client chooses.

Paying for the amount of time the cloud resource is used seems fair, much like the old mainframe time-sharing systems. It basically monitors the amount of time the consumer uses the services and resources and bills for that time according to the predetermined price, so businesses pay only for the time they use the cloud resource. But those who start to use a resource and then do not continue to make full use of it in the allotted time end up paying for more time than they actually use. Enterprises that pay according to the amount of time spent have to be diligent about saturating the use of resources within the time period.

Given that most cloud platforms work with server instances, including storage and compute resources, a new accounting model has emerged that is based on the number of active instances. But for providers, there's a difference between managing 10 VMs with 1 GB of RAM each and managing 1 VM with 10 GB of RAM. And for consumers, not all VMs consume equal hardware resources. Nevertheless, cloud platform providers monitor the number of instances that are spun up and down and charge users accordingly. Thus we can add the following to the list of accounting models:

• according to number of instances

Does that selection of billing models mean that enterprises are happy with how they are billed for consuming resources in the cloud? Not quite. Shared infrastructure, as in the case of cloud computing, is a combination of fixed costs, which include a certain number of startup VMs, and variable costs, which are incremental based on additional VMs. So chargeback models should account for the effect of decreasing marginal costs. Should unused or idle resources be charged? And do you really need all those VMs that are running an OS image on each instance? Cloud containers may seem like a digression, but container technology could provide answers to these questions.

Cloud Containers

To understand cloud containers, we have to begin with LinuX Containers (LXC), which is an operating-system–level virtualization method for running multiple yet isolated Linux systems on a single control host. LXC relies on Linux kernel cgroups to provide virtual environments that have their own process and network spaces, instead of spinning up full-fledged VMs. Improvements in isolation and security have spawned other container technologies, such as Docker, Rocket, Warden, and Virtuozzo. There is even a Google® Container and Amazon EC2® Container Service. So how did we make the leap from LXC to cloud containers?

Note: While LXC is explicitly tied to Linux, new implementations can also support non-Linux systems.

The first generation of cloud container platforms basically do the same thing that physical platforms have done for years: they spin up a server and then load it with a software stack. The difference with cloud platforms is that they take advantage of virtualization techniques. VMs are able to partition and distribute resources within a hypervisor without requiring separate hardware. Until recently it was thought that OS virtualization was the only path to providing isolation for applications running on a server. Figure 5.10 illustrates traditional virtualization.

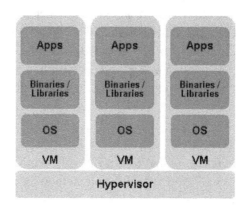

Figure 5.10: Traditional virtualization

Containers offer a different paradigm to cloud platforms by providing a light-weight runtime in isolated and resource-controlled environments without requiring a full-fledged operating system. Each container has its own control group, its own process identifier, and its own namespaces, but containers share the core operating system, binaries, and libraries, as Figure 5.11 shows.

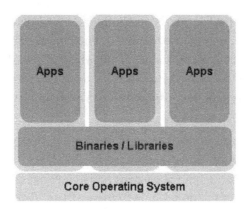

Figure 5.11: Container-based virtualization

Containers offer an alternative to OS-level virtualization while running multiple isolated environments on a single host. In traditional virtualization, VMs might suffer from slow startup times waiting for the OS to boot; in contrast, containers within a single OS are much more efficient. The OS sometimes consumes more memory and disk than the actual application it hosts. Containers decouple provisioning from OS deployment and boot-up. For those very reasons, cloud architects and platform providers are looking at ways of providing container services in the cloud.

The container lifecycle comprises create, configure, use, and destroy, as shown in Figure 5.12. You work with containers primarily by using command-line APIs.

Figure 5.12: Container lifecycle

Because several major IT vendors, including IBM, Google, Red Hat, and Microsoft, have adopted Docker as their container of choice, we focus on Docker here. Docker is an open-source project, the details of which are available at *www.docker .com*. In fact, if you go to that website and click **Install & Docs** to go to the Docker online documentation portal, under **Installation** you'll find an option to install a Docker container on IBM SoftLayer.

Docker essentially automates the deployment of applications inside software containers, which means its scope is at the application level. It uses resource isolation features of the Linux kernel via cgroups and kernel namespaces, thus allowing multiple containers to run within a single Linux instance. But a Docker container is intended to run a single application. If you need to run two distinct applications or services, the recommendation is to use two separate and application-specific Docker containers. Docker was based on LXC, but now it has a new back-end engine named libcontainer. Most Docker container implementations are no longer fully dependent on LXC.

To install Docker, you can follow the installation instructions available for your platform at *docs.docker.com/installation*. If you install Docker on a Microsoft Windows or Apple® Macintosh® workstation, you can start it by using the command

```
boot2docker start
```

You can then run a test of the sample Hello World program by entering the command

```
docker run hello-world
```

When the Docker installation is working correctly, you'll see the message

```
Hello from Docker.
```

An explanation that appears after the Hello message indicates that the Docker daemon does several things:

1. It is contacted by the Docker client.
2. It pulls the "hello-world" image from the Docker Hub.
3. It creates a new container from that image, which runs the executable that produces the output.
4. It streams the output to the Docker client, which sends it to the terminal.

Tip: The default username for boot2docker is docker, and the password is tcuser.

If you type boot2docker on the command line, the usage options will appear. The common options are help, init, restart, status, info, ip, ssh, and upgrade. For example, entering boot2docker info in a terminal window on a Macintosh laptop displays the output shown in Figure 5.13.

```
iMacBookPro:bin admin$ boot2docker info

{

    "Name": "boot2docker-vm",

    "UUID": "356d2b3e-c16a-4d3e-a9dd-b2d087d9a04a",

    "Iso": "/Users/admin/.boot2docker/boot2docker.iso",

    "State": "running",

    "CPUs": 8,

    "Memory": 2048,

    "VRAM": 8,

    "CfgFile": "/Users/admin/VirtualBox VMs/boot2docker-vm/boot2docker-vm.
vbox",

    "BaseFolder": "/Users/admin/VirtualBox VMs/boot2docker-vm",

    "OSType": "",

    "Flag": 0,

    "BootOrder": null,

    "DockerPort": 0,

    "SSHPort": 2022,

    "SerialFile": "/Users/admin/.boot2docker/boot2docker-vm.sock"

}
```

Figure 5.13: Output from the command boot2docker info

As a final example, entering boot2docker ssh in the same terminal window on a Macintosh laptop prints out the Docker logo and opens an SSH session, as you can see in Figure 5.14.

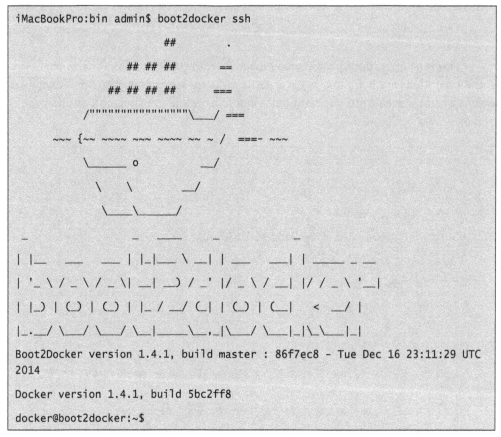

Figure 5.14: Output from the command boot2docker ssh

You should be aware that on Windows® and Macintosh, the latest version of boot2docker sets up a host-only adapter, and the VirtualBox VM's DHCP server will want to connect to 192.168.59.103 on port 2375 or 2376.

There is obviously a lot more to working with and managing containers, building application images, managing data in the containers, and even linking containers together. The overview of Docker presented here is meant simply to whet your appetite to learn more about Docker and other cloud containers.

Cloudlets

Chargeback of IT resources is important to many organizations, and it should be set up after detailed discussions with the help of the cloud service provider. Chargeback in the virtualized world of cloud computing should be dynamic enough to change over time and follow a pricing model that's based on tiered capacity.

This chapter touches upon cloud containers. There are benefits to running containers, but it's only fair to disclose that VMs have a much broader scope because they are scoped to any supported operating system. Hence we see the need for both VMs and containers as choices on every cloud platform.

In Chapter 6 we'll discuss how platforms such as Amazon's AWS and IBM Bluemix are blurring the lines between IaaS and PaaS and between PaaS and SaaS.

This page intentionally left blank.

6

PaaS: Public or Private

A new breed of PaaS platforms offers various software services that can be used to develop and deploy apps. Some of the more popular and well known such cloud platforms are Heroku from Salesforce.com, Amazon Web Services, Microsoft Azure, Google App Engine™, Engine Yard™, and IBM Bluemix. They all run on a hypervisor infrastructure that provides services along with the necessary tooling and applications. Table 6.1 shows some PaaS products and the underlying platform that they take advantage of.

Table 6.1: Some PaaS products and their underlying platform

Bluemix	Engine Yard	Google App Engine	Microsoft Azure	Amazon Web Services	Heroku
Cloud Foundry, SoftLayer	Amazon Web Services	Google Services, KVM	Windows Server 2008, Custom Hyper-V	Elastic Beanstalk, Xen	Amazon Web Services

Although Amazon Web Services is primarily IaaS, it offers many services comparable to PaaS offerings. The underlying concepts of workloads, build tools, integration services, data stores, and management should be common to every PaaS platform. This chapter focuses on IBM's Bluemix platform, which is based on Cloud Foundry™ technology and runs on the IBM SoftLayer infrastructure. (You can find details about Cloud Foundry at http://www.cf.org.)

Discovering Bluemix

Bluemix is IBM's enterprise-grade cloud development and deployment platform—in other words, PaaS. It is hosted on SoftLayer, which is IBM's IaaS. What makes Bluemix "open" is the fact that it's built on top of and is an extension of the Cloud Foundry open-source development and deployment cloud platform. Combining the strength of IBM's software with third-party technologies while using Cloud Foundry to keep it open, Bluemix offers an integrated development experience in the cloud. It helps both born-on-the-cloud and enterprise developers build applications with their choice of tools and languages. Bluemix features cloud integration services that enable a secure connection between an organization's public apps and its private assets.

> **Note:** Bluemix is a constantly evolving platform, and its capabilities, services, and user interface will all change over time. What is captured and discussed here is current as of May 2015.

With nothing to install and no need to configure anything, developers who use Bluemix are able to provision cloud environments almost immediately and accomplish tasks such as composing and hosting Web applications and mobile apps and integrating with back-end systems. Developers can select from a catalog of services to extend their applications. These services are provided by IBM or third-party partners or are obtained from open-source communities.

The fastest way to discover Bluemix is to sign up for a free trial at *console .ng.bluemix.net/solutions/dedicated* and start using it. After you've signed up to use Bluemix and received your credentials, log in.

If you view the catalog after logging in, you'll see a display like that in Figure 6.1 that shows the components that are available on the Bluemix platform. The components are categorized as starters, services, containers, compute, and provider. Starters are sample code that you can build on; alternatively, you can start from scratch. The largest component is Services, which are basically building blocks that you can use to create applications. Compute deals with Cloud Foundry or Docker images. And Provider simply points out the source of the services. There are 12 types of templates, which are listed in Table 6.2.

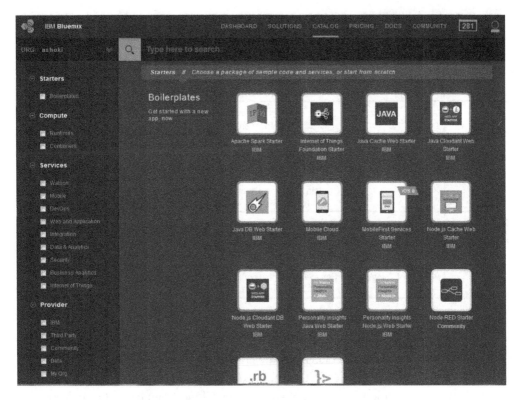

Figure 6.1: Categories of services in Bluemix

Table 6.2: Catalog of services in Bluemix

Category	Templates	Description
Starters	Boilerplates	Get started with a new application. You can choose from Java DB Web Server, Mobile Cloud, and Vaadin Rich Web Starter, among others.
Computer	Runtimes	Run an app in the language of your choice—for example, Node.js, Ruby, or PHP.
	Containers	Create containers from IBM images, or add your own.
Services	Watson	Build cognitive apps that enhance, scale, and accelerate human expertise—for example, language identification, machine translation, and relationship extraction. *Continued*

Category	Templates	Description *Continued*
	Mobile	Quickly start your next mobile app using the likes of Cloudant NoSQL DB, Push, and Twilio.
	DevOps	Move from development to deployment; Delivery Pipeline, BlazeMeter, and Load Impact are some examples.
	Web and Application	Deliver new and mobile apps. Data Cache, MQ Light, Ustream, and Redis are a few of the many available services.
	Integration	Extend existing investments and infrastructure
	Data & Analytics	Services for agile data management and refinement; examples include Cloudant NoSQL DB, and ElephantSQL. Lets you harness the power of data using tools such as BigInsights for Hadoop, dashDB, and Insights for Twitter.
	Security	Build security into application design using AppScan services, including single sign-on
	Business Analytics	Analytics made easy with services for reporting and predictive modeling
	Internet of Things	Services for a new generation of apps that help connect things such as cars and appliances

Working with Bluemix

Once you've created a new app or prepared your application for the cloud, you'll want to know about the new concept of "pushing an app" using Cloud Foundry. When you push an app, all files in the application's project folder, except version control and configuration files, are uploaded to the Cloud Foundry instance. You can create your app by using either the Bluemix user interface or Bluemix DevOps Services. Then you can use the Cloud Foundry command-line utility, cf, to update an app and to create and bind services to the application.

If you were to create an app using the WebSphere Liberty profile, the place to start would be the Liberty for Java Starter Application, a runtime for Bluemix Liberty for Java application development. The WebSphere Application Server Liberty Profile is the container for this type of application. You'll find the starter documentation at *www.ng.bluemix.net/docs/#starters/liberty/index.html#liberty*.

Tip: You can install an Eclipse framework on your desktop to develop apps for Bluemix. The Cloud Foundry (cf) command-line utility is used to push and deploy the app.

Let's use an example to create and deploy a simple Java app.

1. Log on to Bluemix, then go to your dashboard by clicking the **DASHBOARD** menu option.
2. Click the **CREATE AN APP** link in the Applications section, then choose **WEB** as the app template, as shown in Figure 6.2.

Figure 6.2: Choosing an app template

117

3. From the starter apps, choose **Liberty for Java**, as in Figure 6.3, then click **CONTINUE**. It's a good idea to view the Liberty for Java docs before you continue.

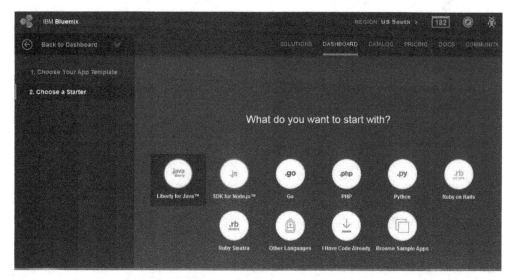

Figure 6.3: Choosing the starter app

4. Type a name for the app, such as MyJavaApp, and click **FINISH**.

The app will start immediately, and the running instance will be displayed in the dashboard, as in Figure 6.4.

Figure 6.4: Dashboard showing the app

If you hover on the link **Your app is running** in the APP HEALTH section on the right, details about the app are displayed.

 Note: If you choose to deploy using an existing server, there will be a pause while the app is deployed.

If you click the geared wheel icon at the top right, you'll see the app-related drop-down menu shown in Figure 6.5, which you can use to stop, restart, rename, or delete the app. Another nifty feature in Bluemix is that you can view the runtime charges for the app and its related services by clicking **Estimate the cost of this app**.

Figure 6.5: The app-related menu

Services, Services, Services

PaaS is all about services that developers can drag and use rather than create from scratch. At this stage you might decide to add a service to your app. Bluemix offers many services that you can add to apps, ranging from data caching to cloud integration and from big data to mobile services. As an example, the Data Cache service improves the performance and user experience of Web applications by retrieving information from fast, managed, in-memory caches, instead of relying on slower disk-based databases.

You'll notice that the Bluemix dashboard (Figure 6.4) contains a box with a plus sign and the link **ADD A SERVICE**. Clicking the link brings up the catalog of services, from which you simply choose the service you want. For this example, let's choose the **Data Cache** service, as shown in Figure 6.6.

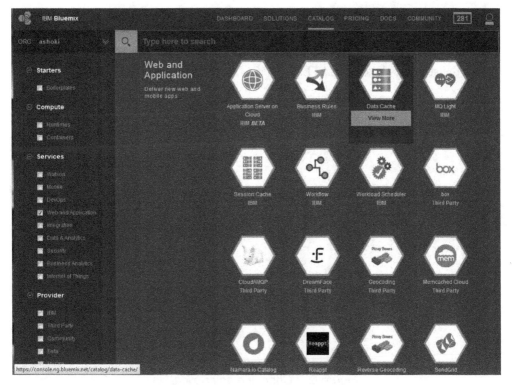

Figure 6.6: Catalog of services

Tip: Most PaaS platforms invite you to try a free trial service. When the trial is over, you have options such as pay-as-you-go and subscription-based service levels. Bluemix offers a "free tier" for all the runtimes and services. If you choose the free tier, you pay only for usage that exceeds the free tier. For more information, refer to the pricing tab on the Bluemix user interface.

After you pick the service, make sure you specify your app from the drop-down menu. We'll choose our sample application, called MyJavaApp, as shown in Figure 6.7. To see details about the service, click **VIEW DOCS**. When you're ready to add the service, click **CREATE**.

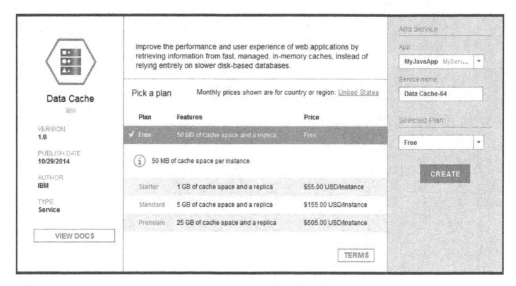

Figure 6.7: Choosing an application

The app pauses for a moment during redeployment, also known as restaging. Look at the dashboard to verify that your app has been restarted. All activity related to the application is logged, as in Figure 6.8.

Figure 6.8: Bluemix dashboard view of an app

In the application navigation pane on the left (Figure 6.9), you'll see menu options related to your app and a list of services that have been added to the app. Click **Start Coding**.

Figure 6.9: The application navigation pane

You'll see the documentation for the Cloud Foundry command-line interface (CLI). Follow the steps to download the cf interface. Then follow the six steps shown in Figure 6.10 to download and extract the starter code so you can modify it and redeploy the app to Bluemix.

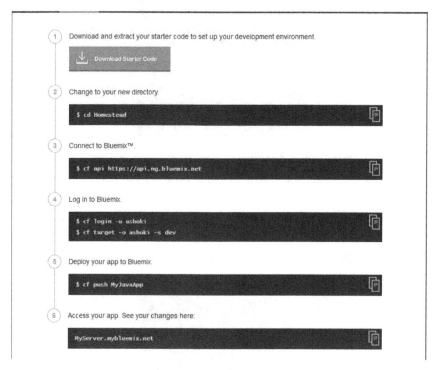

Figure 6.10: App starter code instructions

To see what the default app looks like, you can go to a Web browser and access your app by typing the URL *<host_name>*.*<app_name>*.net. Because the host name in our example is MyServer, the URL for our example would be *myserver.mybluemix .net.* When you enter the URL, you'll see the application welcome screen shown in Figure 6.11.

Figure 6.11: The welcome page of an application running on Bluemix

Now we can change the directory to the downloaded starter application folder and unzip the application zip file (MyJavaApp.zip). The files in the folder include a bin directory, a build.xml file, a src directory, a WebContent directory, and webStarterApp.war.

- The bin directory contains app-related binaries.

- Build.xml allows you to build your app using Ant.

- The src directory contains the server-side Java code. In our sample app, there's just one class: com.ibm.cloudoe.samples.HelloResource.

- The WebContent directory contains the client-side code.

- WebStarterApp.war is the actual application that gets pushed to the Bluemix platform.

If you've downloaded the cf CLI, you can then bring up a command window and log in to the Bluemix environment via the cf tool, as in Figure 6.12. You'll type the command

```
cf login -u <USER_NAME>
```

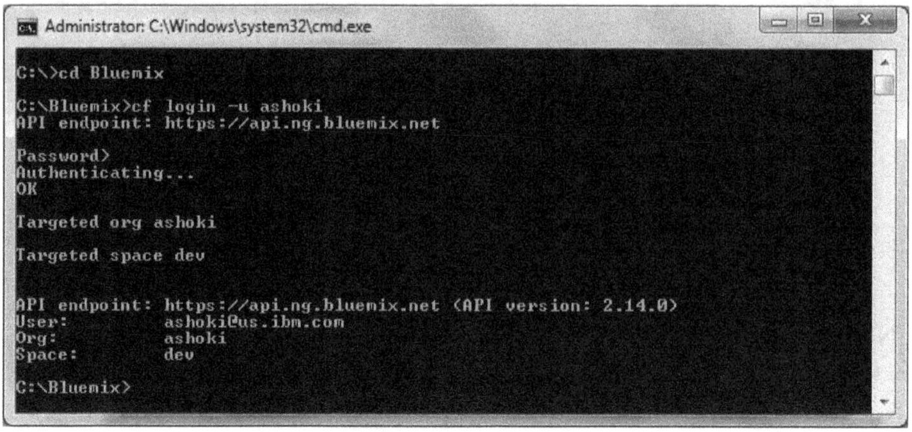

Figure 6.12: cf CLI

After you modify the Java application, you can deploy your modified app to Bluemix using the cf push command. The example below changes the memory to 512 MB.

```
cf push <YOUR_APP_NAME> -p <PATH_TO_APP> -m 512M
```

Using the Service

Now that we know how to add a service to our app and we have the tooling to edit and deploy the app, let's use the Data Cache service as an example. First, take a look at the VCAP_SERVICES environment variable. You can get to it by clicking the **Environment Variables** option on the app-related menu and choosing **VCAP_ SERVICES**. The values are displayed on the dashboard, and you can export them to your workstation as a JSON file. Listing 6.1 shows details about the DataCache service. All data that the application needs to communicate with the service instance can be found in the VCAP_SERVICES environment variable.

```json
{
  "DataCache-1.0" : [ {
    "name" : "Data Cache-64",
    "label" : "DataCache-1.0",
    "plan" : "free",
    "credentials" : {
      "catalogEndPoint" : "192.155.240.162:2809,192.155.240.163:2809",
      "restResource" :
"http://192.155.240.162/resources/datacaches/sW0aDPjdQ7ymsLgAjyKMuwAZ",
      "restResourceSecure" :
"https://ecaas63.ng.bluemix.net/resources/datacaches/
sW0aDPjdQ7ymsLgAjyKMuwAZ",
      "gridName" : "sW0aDPjdQ7ymsLgAjyKMuwAZ",
      "username" : "75kcCCF2SAidv9LcxcZQMAIK",
      "password" : "OHJU4xADQTSJOSDwIHSkKgJO"
    }
  } ]
}
```

Listing 6.1: VCAP_SERVICES content

In your application code, you'll have to parse VCAP_SERVICES to obtain the Data Cache connection information, which is shown in Figure 6.13.

```
Map env = System.getenv();
String vcap = env.get("VCAP_SERVICES");
JSONObject obj = new JSONObject(vcap);
String[] names = JSONObject.getNames(obj);
if (names != null) {
    for (String name : names) {
        if (name.startsWith("DataCache")) {
            JSONArray val = obj.getJSONArray(name);
            JSONObject serviceAttr = val.getJSONObject(0);
            JSONObject credentials = serviceAttr.getJSONObject("credentials");

            username = credentials.getString("username");
            password = credentials.getString("password");
            endpoint=credentials.getString("catalogEndPoint");
            gridName= credentials.getString("gridName");

            break;
        }
    }
}
```

Figure 6.13: Service connection information

After you get the connection information, you can use it to connect to the Data Cache service and create a session by using IBM WebSphere Extreme Scale APIs, as in Figure 6.14.

```
ObjectGridManager ogm = ObjectGridManagerFactory.getObjectGridManager();
ClientSecurityConfiguration csc=null;
csc=ClientSecurityConfigurationFactory.getClientSecurityConfiguration();
csc.setCredentialGenerator(new UserPasswordCredentialGenerator(username,password));
csc.setSecurityEnabled(true);

ClientClusterContext ccc = ogm.connect(endpoint, csc, null);
ObjectGrid clientGrid = ogm.getObjectGrid(ccc, gridName);
ogSession = clientGrid.getSession();
```

Figure 6.14: Service connection using APIs

This is just one simple illustration of the DevOps feature that Bluemix and other such PaaS platforms provide. Some code snippets are provided here, but you can get all the details about the Data Cache service at *www.ng.bluemix.net/docs/#services/DataCache/index.html.*

Whether you're creating Java apps or Node.js apps, adding, deploying, and testing the apps is almost instantaneous. And when you're satisfied with the results, you can make the app publicly available with just a few more clicks.

Private PaaS

Thus far it's been easy to visualize IT solutions featuring public PaaS. But can customers get all the features of public PaaS to run within their IT confines—in other words, as a private PaaS? In fact, PaaS vendors now offer exactly that: a private PaaS. The single most sought-after feature for such offerings is security. A private PaaS offers all the benefits of a public PaaS while meeting enterprise security and privacy requirements.

A private PaaS complies with all corporate IT security requirements because it is exclusive to your enterprise and hosted on your private cloud, which operates behind your firewall. A private PaaS lets you control where your data is stored. Healthcare organizations, financial institutions, and other enterprises that collect personal private information can now safeguard this sensitive information within the confines of their IT walls while offering developers ease of development and deployment and the other self-service capabilities they often demand.

One other benefit that comes with hosting private PaaS but is often overlooked is customization. While most public PaaS platforms take a one-size-fits-all approach, a private PaaS lets you integrate it within your existing IT infrastructure and customize it to support the environments and languages that your developers use.

Some of the players in this space are Apprenda; Stackato, which uses Cloud Foundry; WSO2, which is built on top of Apache Stratos; and IBM's own Bluemix. The on-premises version of Bluemix is known as Bluemix Local, and customers can also have their own slice of public Bluemix, known as Bluemix Dedicated.

Bluemix Dedicated is your own single-tenant Bluemix environment, hosted in an isolated SoftLayer instance and managed by IBM. It addresses all the issues alluded to earlier, such as corporate security policy, data residency, and privacy. A key component of Bluemix Dedicated is the connection it shares to the public cloud instance of Bluemix. Developers can pull in APIs and services from public Bluemix and use those capabilities in apps that might be running on Bluemix Dedicated.

All these private PaaS platforms operate on a layered architecture, where the layers typically are IaaS and a middleware framework topped off by services and a SaaS model. Figure 6.15, taken from *docs.wso2.com/display/PP400/Architecture*, depicts WSO2's private PaaS layered architecture, which is built on top of the Apache Stratos project.

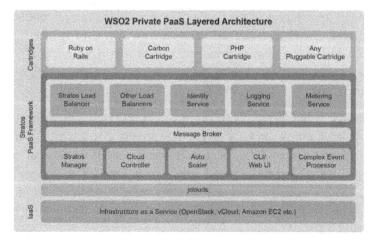

Figure 6.15: WSO2 private PaaS layered architecture

Overview of Bluemix Dedicated

Bluemix Dedicated is single-tenant hardware—that is, an enterprise's own dedicated SoftLayer environment that's securely connected to both public Bluemix and the enterprise's own data center. Since Bluemix Dedicated connects to a customer's network either directly or via VPN, the benefits of such a setup are threefold: it is secure, it is fast, and best of all, access is unmetered. Bluemix Dedicated is also integrated with the customer's LDAP server, which allows for control over who can access the environment. And Bluemix Dedicated is a hosted managed cloud service: IBM manages the platform and all the dedicated services.

As in all hosted managed services, there is nothing for the customer to set up. The instance is deployed by the provider with redundancy for each component; thus there is no single point of failure. Once you sign up, the platform provider creates the environment that was requested, and you as a consumer are given access information. Upgrades and maintenance are handled by the provider and are scheduled at your convenience.

The public Bluemix platform and Bluemix Dedicated runtimes and services are hosted on the same SoftLayer data center that is totally dedicated to a particular customer. That arrangement does not make it a hybrid cloud solution, however. The customer still has the ability to connect to all multi-tenant services in the public catalog. All connections are secured, and most important, sensitive data is kept private behind the customer's firewall. There is also a new private API catalog that allows for connecting securely to on-premises data. Consequently, developers can securely and seamlessly connect data from back-end systems of record to systems of engagement, such as mobile and social applications.

Figure 6.16 shows how Bluemix Dedicated is set up. Notice the secure connection between public Bluemix and Bluemix Dedicated; it's used for maintenance of Bluemix Dedicated and for service provisioning and life cycle tasks in public Bluemix. The VPN or direct connection to the customer's data center allows developers to push and debug apps, lets applications invoke enterprise services, and provides the ability to configure and use the corporate LDAP. Going forward, we will see the emergence of technologies that will allow us to distribute components across dedicated, local, and public infrastructure.

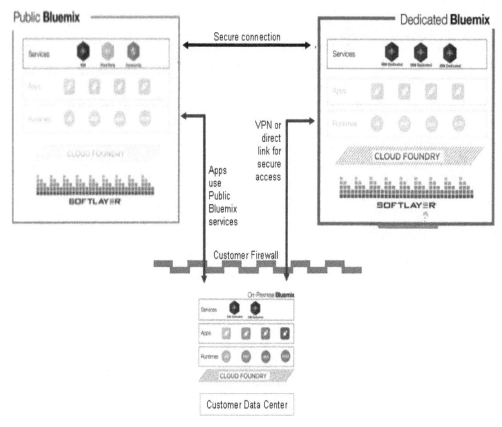

Figure 6.16: Bluemix Dedicated topology

Bluemix and Container Service

In Chapter 5 we introduced cloud containers. PaaS providers have been quick to adopt the container model, and Bluemix is headed in that direction as well. If you go to the Bluemix catalog and look in the Integration section, as in Figure 6.17, you'll see that Containers are now available. These services help you seamlessly integrate Cloud Foundry or Docker containers into your app development activities.

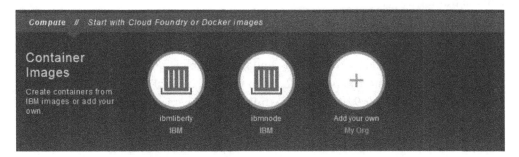

Figure 6.17: Container service in Bluemix

The documentation states that the IBM Containers service enables you to run Docker containers in a hosted cloud environment on Bluemix. You can port your existing applications to Bluemix and make them publicly accessible by using containers. A private registry is provided where trusted images can be uploaded, stored, and retrieved.

 Note: You need IBM Containers Extension (ICE), to run IBM Containers Service on Bluemix.

Cloudlets

Although this chapter started out discussing public PaaS, it progressed through the benefits of private PaaS and almost ended up discussing hybrid cloud. It has become clear to enterprises deploying cloud solutions that maintaining control over some of their data and using common services in a public cloud gives them the best of both worlds. Such a solution addresses security, scalability, and rapid development while still controlling costs.

When you have a private cloud or an on-premises resource that exchanges data with the public cloud or off-premises services, you end up with a hybrid cloud environment, and that is exactly what most vendors are pursuing—a hybrid cloud solution that utilizes both private and public clouds to perform distinct functions. We'll cover hybrid clouds in Chapter 9. In the meanwhile, here are some references you might want to check out.

- Bluemix Developers Community: *developer.ibm.com/bluemix/*

- Bluemix documentation: *www.ng.bluemix.net/docs/*

- WSO2 Private PaaS: *wso2.com/cloud/private-paas/*

- Apache Stratos Project: *stratos.apache.org/*

7

Operational Transformation

The biggest changes that cloud computing brings to an enterprise are changes in mindset and operational transformation. While some of these changes are abstract, there are very concrete things that IT organizations can and should do to take full advantage of the cloud environment. From redefining roles to taking on new responsibilities, this chapter discusses the various operational and organizational transformations afoot in large IT organizations.

In this chapter we discuss the actors defined in IBM's Cloud Computing Reference Architecture (CCRA). We also list and describe the new roles and corresponding responsibilities that cloud platforms, such as PureApplication System and Bluemix, bring about. Even signing up to be a user of public cloud services, whether those services are infrastructure or software, requires a change in the IT thought process. By the end of this chapter, it should be apparent that to operate in this new environment you need to be more of a generalist than a specialist.

IT Roles in Cloud Computing

The International Organization for Standardization (ISO) recently published the cloud computing reference architecture that it has adopted at *standards.iso.org/ittf/Publicly AvailableStandards/c060545_ISO_IEC_17789_2014.zip*. Much of the content regarding roles and use cases came from IBM's CCRA. There are three common, well-established roles in cloud computing:

- **Cloud service provider**—an organization or a vendor that hosts the cloud and provides cloud services. The cloud service provider manages the computing infrastructure required to provide the services, runs the cloud software that provides the services, and delivers the cloud services through secure network access.

- **Cloud service consumer**—enterprises or individuals that request, pay for, and consume cloud services. The cloud service consumer browses the service catalog from the cloud service provider, requests the desired service, agrees to a service contract with the provider, and uses the service.

- **Cloud service broker or partner**—businesses that offer supporting services for the cloud.

The NIST CCRA lists cloud auditor as another major role. A cloud auditor is someone who audits the cloud service and its implementation, performance, and security.

All of these roles have sub-roles, which are shown in Figure 7.1 but are not described in detail here because most organizations already have their own variation of those roles. At a high level, all activities, such as selecting a cloud partner, purchasing cloud services, user provisioning, providing network connectivity, administering tenancies, performing backup and recovery, monitoring the service, billing, and providing usage reports are the responsibility of one or more of the sub-roles.

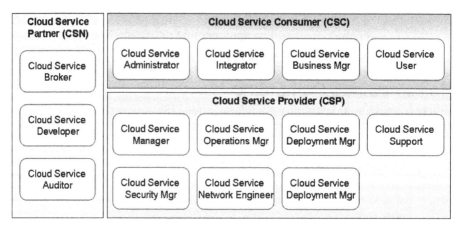

Figure 7.1: Roles and sub-roles within cloud computing

When it comes to services, the key to receiving good service is to form a good business relationship with the service provider. Cloud services are no different. The cloud service consumer should forge a good relationship with the cloud service provider, and both should agree on a strong service-level agreement.

It is quite possible that if you drill down into any of the deployment models, you may find certain specific roles or actors. For example, Figure 7.2 shows the PaaS actors from the IBM CCRA. Depending on which deployment model is offered or serviced, the roles might vary a bit. If you sign up for SaaS, as a consumer you get very little if any control of the environment. If you choose PaaS, you get some control over the environment because PaaS has to provide for development and deployment of applications, for which you would need development tools and possibly access to the underlying network, operating system, and storage. And in the case of IaaS, the consumer gets quite a bit of control. Regardless of the level of service a consumer purchases, a scope of control should be agreed upon between the consumer and the provider.

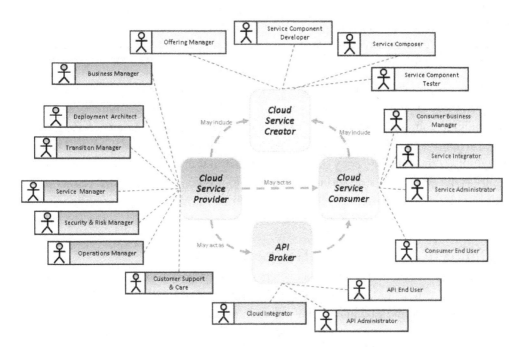

Figure 7.2: Actors in the PaaS discipline from the IBM CCRA

The cloud service consumer might choose to request service from a cloud broker instead of contacting a cloud provider directly. In that case, the number of people the consumer deals with directly is drastically reduced. The cloud broker would manage the use, performance, and delivery of all cloud services and even negotiate the business relationship between cloud provider and cloud consumer.

As we've seen, the cloud service provider and the cloud service consumer have differing degrees of control over the computing resources in the cloud environment. The recommendation is for both to collaboratively design, build, and operate cloud-based systems, which is quite different from traditional IT systems, in which one organization has control over the entire stack of computing resources. We'll discuss this further a bit later.

First, though, one other topic should be mentioned, and that is cloud service management. Management includes all service-related functions necessary for the management and operation of the services promised or offered to the consumer. It mainly entails business support systems, and to some degree portability and interoperability. From a business support systems perspective, cloud service management includes all the components needed to run client-facing business operations, such as contract management, inventory management, pricing, accounting and billing, and reporting and auditing.

As far as portability is concerned, cloud service consumers want to know whether they can move their data or applications across multiple cloud environments and have the ability to communicate between multiple clouds. It behooves cloud service providers to support data portability, service interoperability, and system portability. Data portability is the ability to copy data objects into or out of a cloud. Service interoperability is the ability of cloud service consumers to use their data and services across multiple clouds. And system portability is the ability to migrate applications and services from one service provider to another. These features are not easily supported.

A Different Approach to IT Operations

IT staff who manage traditional data centers have far more control than those who manage cloud environments. The nature of cloud computing allows non-IT staff to do more, so the traditional install-and-maintain paradigm has given way to deploy and monitor. As the move to service-based IT continues, the knowledge, skills, and abilities of many of the IT roles are very quickly being transformed.

As Figure 7.3 shows, in a traditional data center IT staff has full control over most components and tasks. But as you move to "as a service" environments, we see the IT teams have less control of and influence over how things are done. While that might make IT operations teams uneasy, it bodes well for the developer community because they are no longer at the mercy of the IT staff and can thus accelerate the speed of development and deployment of software solutions.

	Physical Servers	Storage	Network	Operating System	Middleware	Applications
SaaS	⊘	⊘	⊘	⊘	⊘	●
PaaS	⊘	⊘	⊘	◉	◉	●
IaaS	●	●	●	◉	⊘	⊘
Traditional Data Center	●	●	●	●	●	◉

● Full Control   ◉ Partial Control   ⊘ No Control

Figure 7.3: Spheres of influence by IT departments

This shift really means that the roles, responsibilities, and skill sets are changing in the IT landscape. For example, system administrators now have the opportunity to become cloud administrators; service managers can look ahead to becoming cloud service managers; enterprise architects are becoming cloud architects; and even the ever-present computer consultant can add new skills to his or her repertoire and become a cloud consultant. So there is something new for everyone in the cloud space.

New Opportunities in Cloud Computing

What do IT professionals have to look forward to in moving to the cloud? The first thing to realize is that systems have become smarter, simpler, and more accessible, and consequently the need is for more generalists and fewer specialists in the cloud-based IT organization. The expert integrated systems or converged systems on which most cloud environments run are forcing organizations to become less compartmentalized and much more integrated.

These cloud systems are also forcing a change in skill sets. One has to think about transient resources more than permanent resources. The promise of making it easier to implement virtualized environments also means that re-provisioning the same resources becomes easier. The result is that environments have shorter lifetimes. People will have to become good at learning various abstraction layers.

Some of the new roles and the responsibilities that come with them are discussed below. These roles are directly responsible for interacting with cloud systems. Other roles are more consultative in nature and are considered secondary roles. Figure 7.4 captures the suggested roles for IT departments that are considering implementing cloud solutions.

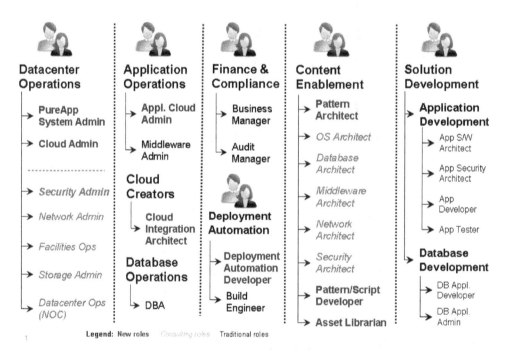

Figure 7.4: Suggested roles for IT departments deploying cloud solutions

- **Cloud administrator**—The cloud administrator role is responsible for configuring and managing the physical cloud. That responsibility encompasses all assets related to the cloud, such as creating cloud groups to provide isolation, creating IP groups when required, monitoring resource utilization, and most important, adjusting assigned resources based on the needs and demands of the cloud users.

- **Cloud architect**—It is imperative that enterprise architects now understand IaaS, PaaS, and SaaS. Every cloud computing architecture will touch one or more of those services. Knowing whether to recommend a public cloud or a private cloud and whether to make use of Software as a Service (SaaS) for lower environments are some of the nuances that cloud architects must be familiar with. A cloud architect will also be asked to provide leadership in convincing customers on the adoption and use of cloud computing.

- **Cloud consultant**—The things that drive cloud computing, such as rapid application development and continuous delivery or DevOps, new scripting languages, and new APIs, including Representational State Transfer (REST) and mobile APIs, are some of the competencies a cloud consultant needs to develop. Whether it is automating deployments or pushing applications to a public cloud platform, this role forces one to be a generalist and agile.

- **Cloud developer**—A cloud developer has a narrower scope than does a cloud consultant. He or she would create applications using languages such as Node.js and use Python or shell scripting to facilitate application deployment. The cloud developer would know how to grab resources in the cloud when needed and make it a point to release them or de-allocate them they are no longer needed. One has to understand the intricacies of working in a shared environment and why security is so important.

- **Cloud integration architect**—Developing integration architecture and providing integration solution guidance is the main role of the cloud integration architect. Whether it's integration of back-end systems in the data center with the public cloud or finding the right architecture to connect an on-premises cloud with off-premises services, the cloud integration architect would be familiar with all types of cloud, especially hybrid cloud solutions. This role would also need to be aware of cloud orchestration and related tools, as illustrated in Figure 7.5.

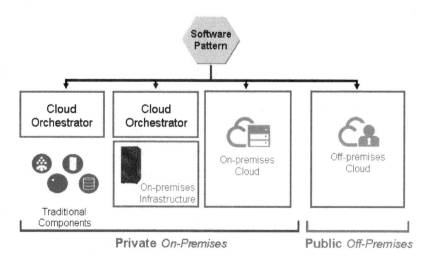

Figure 7.5: Knowledge scope for a cloud integration architect

Other roles are not new, but their job descriptions have expanded to include cloud-related responsibilities.

- **System administrator**—As with any physical server, the system administrator will have to own the physical cloud system in the case of a private or on-premises cloud. Keeping the system up, monitoring it, reporting on it, and providing security credentials to users would be among the system administrator's tasks. If the organization is using a public cloud or off-premises cloud, the additional responsibilities would be minimal and would entail monitoring the availability of the off-premises cloud, requesting user and group access, and requesting new software.

- **Network administrator**—The job of planning, design, assigning, deploying, and maintaining the enterprise network continues as usual, but now the job would span one or more cloud infrastructures. Network administrators would have to work with the cloud administrator to agree on the allocation of network resources and provide the necessary VLANs and IP groups to create clouds and ensure network compliance within the enterprise.

- **Security administrator**—One area that garners a lot of attention is security. Clients are afraid that putting things on the cloud would open a window into all their business secrets and private data. Security administrators are heavily consulted when standing up a cloud environment to enforce corporate security compliance and appease corporate executives that there are no security holes that would allow unauthorized entry into the corporate IT domain from the cloud. While customers love the idea of self-service, security administrators have to constantly manage users and groups and review the necessary authorization to the cloud.

The roles of application developer and application tester continue to be necessary in the cloud environment but are not included here because they haven't changed. The final set of roles is specific to using IBM's PureApplication System as the private cloud platform.

- **Pattern architect**—Defining, designing, and, most important, deciding whether to use an existing pattern or create a new pattern are some of the tasks the pattern architect performs. Pattern architects work with pattern developers to ensure that best practices are followed and that patterns are fully documented and coded in such a way that the components can be reused or shared across multiple environments. The pattern architect also consults with the security administrator to ensure that corporate standards for OS hardening and security are satisfied.

- **Pattern developer**—The pattern developer works closely with the pattern architect. Also known as the script developer, this person is responsible for creating patterns and script packages that can be deployed on PureApplication Systems. More often than not, he or she ends up modifying or customizing out-of-the-box patterns. From a life cycle perspective, this person is also responsible for updating and maintaining the patterns and related artifacts.

- **Asset manager**—The asset manager or asset librarian manages all artifacts (hypervisor images, patterns, script packages, plug-ins, and shared services) across the organization. Asset managers make sure that the PureApplication System catalog is kept current and the correct versions are stored in a version control system. Maintaining different versions of the artifacts for various environments—development, test, and production—can be quite a responsibility.

- **Project manager**—It would be an omission not to mention the new responsibilities for project managers who have to manage cloud projects. The title might not change, but anyone who is responsible for managing cloud projects has to shed old-school ways and learn to be agile. Project management in the cloud is an iterative and incremental method of managing the design, build, and deployment of cloud projects. The project manager must be flexible and communicate readily and effectively with both the development team and the customer. The most important principle of cloud projects is to satisfy the customer through early and continuous delivery of working pieces of software.

Resiliency

In IT, we commonly use the phrases 24 x 7, always up, and zero downtime when referring to the availability of computer systems. In cloud parlance, the term resiliency is used because we know that disruptions happen and that what really matters is the system's ability to recover from an outage and continue serving its purpose. Finding the root cause and fixing the outage or disruption is secondary. One survey of 200 data centers by *USA Today* and another study by Uptime Institute have reported that the average hourly cost of downtime is close to $100,000. The terms recovery time objective (RTO) and recovery point objective (RPO) still apply. But when virtualized environments such as the cloud are paired with physical servers, cloud providers are better prepared to meet shortened RTOs, and that is where the effective use of public and hybrid clouds comes in.

Companies such as IBM are opening up resiliency centers that integrate cloud and traditional IT disaster recovery capabilities with physical security features. Many such cloud service providers now measure recovery time in minutes rather than hours. Businesses now focus on a concept called business continuity, which is not the same thing as disaster recovery. Business continuity is the capability of an organization to continue delivering products or services at acceptable levels in the wake of a disaster or impedance.

Resiliency centers are open 24 hours a day, seven days a week, with teams monitoring potential disaster events. They are equipped to mobilize as needed to ensure that the infrastructure that supports the cloud is configured to handle any and all kinds of threats. At the very core these IT centers are there to make good on the promise to keep data, applications, transactions, and eventually people secure.

As a case in point, by the end of 2015 IBM will have 17 global centers running the SoftLayer infrastructure and 150 resiliency centers all geared to speeding up recovery times by virtually eliminating network latency. And more are planned.

Any discussion of cloud environment resiliency would not be complete without mentioning Recovery as a Service (RaaS) or Disaster Recovery as a Service (DRaaS). The technology that powers disaster recovery has become efficient and affordable and will continue to become more capable as businesses get better at recovery. DRaaS is a predetermined set of processes that vendors offer clients to develop and implement a failover or recovery plan in the event of a disaster.

Retooling and Re-skilling of IT Personnel

A critical aspect of operational transformation is retooling of existing IT personnel. We IT professionals have heard over the past couple of years how important it is for us to retool our skills for the cloud. Similarly, it is imperative for enterprises to encourage their IT staff to retool their skill set for the cloud and to rethink existing IT processes. While the paradigm shift is dramatic, the transition from a traditional IT environment to a cloud computing environment does not have to be daunting.

The focus should be to help staff improve their skills and progress in a manner that will benefit their individual careers in the long run. Leaving improvement of skills to self-learning is not always the best solution. After everyone has had an initial cloud basics class onsite, they can continue learning at their own pace. The underlying message to the entire IT staff should be that they will not be losing their jobs but that they need to embrace the new, faster, more agile paradigm, and that collaboration is key. They might have to accept and learn new tools and be willing to cede some control to automation. New approaches to solving IT problems will also be required. Staff members should all select areas of specialization and be encouraged to pursue certifications. Online training courses, plenty of documentation, demos, white papers, and other resources are readily available on various Internet sites, and some are even free.

Cloud computing has affected some traditional IT jobs more than others. The three IT jobs that have been impacted the most are application developers, because they have to learn new languages and frameworks and learn to build elastic applications; system administrators, because many tasks are being automated and system administrators must cede control of IT resources in the cloud; and architects, who now have to be more of a generalist than a specialist and learn about networking, storage, and virtualization.

As much as cloud computing transforms traditional IT operations and roles, many activities continue to be the same, which helps in the transition. But cloud computing also transforms processes.

Process Transformation

The final piece of operational transformation is transformation of processes, be they existing IT processes within an enterprise or approval processes for consumers wanting to use IT services. Consumers, whether they are enterprise employees who need computing resources or consumers in the marketplace who want to sign up for new service, can now access cloud services via self-service portals. One result is that six process-transformation trends have become evident.

- Developers no longer need to interact with IT engineering or IT operations groups to acquire environments. Rather, developers are directed to a kiosk or website to enter their request. Certain requests, depending on the scope of resources requested, still may require approval, but even that is automated to a certain degree. No matter how it happens, IT operations will always want to know what resources are used, what they're used for, and who uses them in order to allocate cost.

- In the cloud parlance of spinning up new environments, the mentality has changed from "repair it" to "redeploy it." There are trade-offs in that spectrum. While discarding environments and redeploying them usually works for non-production environments, it doesn't work for production environments. A classic example is that we don't bother to make backups of much of anything on the application server tier of VMs. We might keep log files for auditing purposes, but that's about it. If something bad happens to an application server VM, we deploy a new one; we don't try to restore from backup. Again, this scenario is not workable in a production environment.

- Another variation is evident with regard to reusing test environments, which works very well in the cloud. In this case, the move is away from cleaning up environments to redeploying them. For example, say that test team A uses an environment and finishes up, then test team B comes along and needs an environment. Traditionally, the existing environment would somehow be "scrubbed" of the effects of test team A and handed over to test team B. However, artifacts would inevitably remain in the environment from the presence of test team A. Working within the cloud framework, it is much more convenient to delete the old test environment and deploy a brand new one. And it doesn't take much time, either.

- Another major process transformation is thinking of infrastructure as code and treating it as such, applying source-code management and first-class software development principles. That means using newer and better development tooling and frameworks, such as Puppet, Chef, Salt, and libraries of reusable modules. Even the scripting languages, such as Python/Jython and Ruby, are dramatically more powerful. Infrastructure setup used to be done using long, archaic processes on a first-come, first-served basis, or in some cases was ad hoc. Now processes are defined and agile.

- With the ability to rapidly deploy environments, software development and test teams are provided environments more readily, which lets them do more testing with more realistic topologies. It also becomes easier for the operations team to experiment with different combinations of process deployments to make optimal use of resources for various performance targets. A simple example is including a messaging provider (queue manager) on the same machine with each application server or sharing a remote messaging provider among several application servers.

- Finally, IT organizations and their users will challenge many manual processes. Service-level agreements (SLAs) will have to be modified because deploying physical environments now happens in minutes or hours at most rather than days or weeks. While IT departments and strategic out-sourcing service providers are willing to rework SLAs, there are speed bumps such as dealing with firewall rule changes, waiting for IP addresses, and security scans of deployed VMs that require some form of human verification. Although there are no ready answers for wringing this overhead out of the process, it is something to be aware of.

Cloudlets

The best approach to the cloud-related IT transformation is not to fight it or fear it, but to embrace it and learn as much as you can. The cloud is here to stay, and changes will be ongoing. People and companies that adapt to the changes will find themselves in a stronger position in the future.

The biggest benefit of a private cloud environment, although it may not be obvious at the outset, is that it results in less work for IT personnel. System administrators no longer have to continually rack and stack servers; the virtualized infrastructure does not need constant care; and even network cabling and storage management is done just once, during setup. And that is a transformation any organization will welcome.

References

- International Organization for Standardization/International Electrotechnical Commission (ISO/IEC) Cloud Computing Reference Architecture: *standards .iso.org/ittf/PubliclyAvailableStandards/c060545_ISO_IEC_17789_2014.zip*

- NIST Cloud Computing Reference Architecture: *www.nist.gov/manuscript-publication-search.cfm?pub_id=909505*

- Organizational structure in PureApplication System operations: *www.ibm .com/developerworks/websphere/techjournal/1307_brown2/1307_brown2 .html*

- Introduction to Salt: *docs.saltstack.com/en/latest/*

8

Cloud Orchestration

The growth of virtualized environments has created a new opportunity for service providers to create those environments. The process of creating an environment, whether it is simply deployment of a virtual machine (VM) or specific placement and management of workloads, is commonly known as *orchestration* or *service orchestration*. Creating virtualized servers is not new in the distributed world of service-oriented architecture, but in the cloud domain specialized software can help create or deploy environments, including even on-premises systems. In the simplest of terms, cloud orchestration lets you fully utilize a cloud platform.

The term *orchestration* originally referred to the arrangement and coordination of individual musical instruments for a given composition. Cloud orchestration plays an analogous role by automating and bringing together the configuration, coordination, and management of software services to form a cloud environment. Whether you need to manage server runtimes, back up and restore systems and applications, or manage applications, orchestration in the cloud has to be able to achieve the objectives across heterogeneous systems in multiple locations.

The path to delivering a defined cloud service requires first combining and arranging the architecture, tools, and processes to form the structure of the service. Then, software and hardware components need to be stitched together and put into place on the underlying structure. Finally, workflows must be connected and automated when applicable. Cloud orchestration assists in all these tasks, enabling a service development project that used to take weeks or months to be completed in a matter of days.

Cloud orchestration is crucial to the delivery of cloud services because the cloud is all about scale, fulfillment assurance, and accurate billing. Achieving these objectives entails workflows in various technical and business domains, and specifically automated workflows.

Both commercial and open-source cloud orchestration tools are available. Products include vCenter Orchestrator from VMware, IBM Cloud Orchestrator (ICO), SkySight from Capgemini, Flexiant™ Cloud Orchestrator, and the highly popular open-source tools Chef and Puppet. This chapter discusses ICO and wraps up with an overview of the cloud infrastructure configuration tool Chef.

Overview of IBM Cloud Orchestrator

Based on OpenStack®, IBM Cloud Orchestrator is used to quickly deliver and manage cloud services both on and off premises. Cloud orchestration products use workflows to connect various processes and associated resources. ICO uses the workflow engine from IBM Business Process Manager (BPM) and integrates with existing environments using APIs and tooling extensions.

The PureApplication System patterns discussed in Chapter 3 on are also used within ICO. Figure 8.1 illustrates how the pattern engine is embedded in the ICO platform. Because ICO is built with the IBM CCRA in mind, it is an open and secure solution that meets privacy and governance guidelines. The ICO platform can support deployments on a broad range of hypervisors, including Amazon EC2, VMware, IBM System z®, PowerVM®, OpenStack, and kernel-based virtual machines (KVM). OpenStack deserves special mention because it is a free, open-source set of software tools used for building and managing computing software platforms for public and private clouds. ICO makes full use of OpenStack in the IaaS layer with Nova (OpenStack's distributed computing component), Neutron (OpenStack's "networking as a service" project), and the block storage service Cinder.

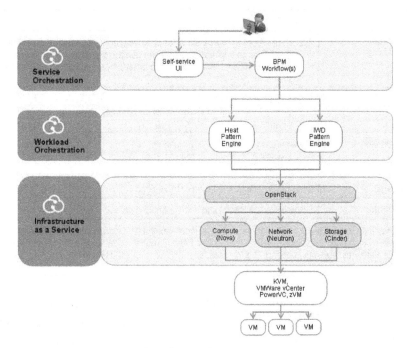

Figure 8.1: IBM Cloud Orchestration platform

ICO is available in two editions: IBM Cloud Orchestrator and IBM Cloud Orchestrator Enterprise Edition, which includes monitoring and cost management. This chapter focuses on the basic ICO. Table 8.1 gives a brief description of the role of each major ICO component.

Table 8.1: ICO components

ICO Component	Role
Infrastructure as a Service	Manages access to compute, storage, and networking resources in the virtual environment. All requests to provision services across these resources are performed by this component. The IaaS component is delivered by using OpenStack.
Software stacks	When a virtual system is deployed, you can specify multiple software packages to be deployed when you first bring up the system. *Continued*

ICO Component	Role	*Continued*
Patterns	Predefined topologies that allow for deploying complex middleware configurations and multi-node applications. One can use the graphical editor to describe multiple virtual systems, each with a base image and set of software to be installed.	
Workflow orchestration	A graphical editor that lets the user easily customize and extend procedures after a user request is initiated. Workflow orchestration also provides facilities to customize the self-service catalog.	
Self-service catalog	A website where one can download various forms of automation resources for use within ICO, including ready-to-use patterns, images, and references to automation communities such as Chef.	
Service management	Optional additional management functions included in ICO Enterprise Edition.	
Development tools	Other developer tools, such as continuous delivery tools, that can be integrated.	
Note: ICO uses the OpenStack orchestration service, specifically the native OpenStack Heat Orchestration Templates (known by the acronym HOT). These OpenStack templates enable creation of resource types such as instances, volumes, floating IP addresses, security groups, and users. Once created, the resources are referred to as *stacks*.		

ICO uses templates, or patterns, from OpenStack, in particular some of the same patterns that are used in IBM PureApplication System. But ICO also supports other engines, specifically OpenStack Heat and the single virtual server OpenStack Nova. Table 8.2 enumerates some of the differences between ICO-supported pattern engines.

Table 8.2: Pattern engines supported in ICO

	Single Server – Nova	Stacks – Heat	Patterns – IBM Workload Deployer
Complexity	Simple	Intermediate	Complex
Purpose	Single VM	Multiple VMs with network and storage	Multiple VMs with network, storage, and additional software
Supported Hypervisors	All	All except ICO's Public Cloud Gateway	All
Note: ICO supports OASIS Topology and Orchestration Specification for Cloud Applications (TOSCA). TOSCA enables the consumption of third-party content provided in a standardized format.			

Four main components must be installed when setting up ICO. In order of their installation, those components are the deployment server, which hosts the deployment service; central servers, which host the core management components; region servers, which communicate with the hypervisor infrastructure; and compute nodes provided by KVM.

Figure 8.2 depicts a deployment topology based on VMware. Four central servers form the manage-from environment, and a fifth VM, by way of the region server, acts as the interface between the manage-from environment and the manage-to environment. Each region server hosts OpenStack (OS) Nova, the compute service; Glance, an image service that provides a catalog and repository for virtual disk images; Cinder, a storage block service that provides persistent block storage to guest VMs; Heat, the infrastructure orchestration service; and qpid, the messaging system leveraged by the OpenStack services. If you want to use OpenStack Neutron to provide network management services, you must install Neutron on a dedicated system. The

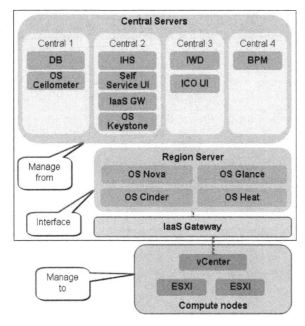

Figure 8.2: ICO topology with VMware

IBM Knowledge Center (*www-01.ibm.com/support/knowledgecenter/SS4KMC_2.4.0/ com.ibm.sco.doc_2.4/c_install_scenarios.html*) lists various supported deployment topologies, including distributed high-availability topologies.

Before installing the ICO software, you must ensure that all the central servers can communicate with each other and that the region server can communicate with the VMware ESX® server. Verify the contents of the configuration file (central-server.cfg) and run deploy_central_server.sh to install the central servers. Then create the region server database, verify the other configuration file (region-server.cfg), and run deploy_region_server.sh. Chef is used to deploy all the components shown in Figure 8.2.

Working with IBM Cloud Orchestrator

Assuming the ICO environment has been set up and you have credentials to access it, you can bring up a Web browser, go to the URL, and log in. Then, if you go to **SELF-SERVICE CATALOG**, you'll see a display similar to that in Figure 8.3 showing the available services.

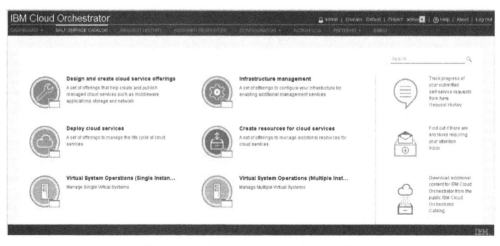

Figure 8.3: Self-service catalog in ICO

Let's choose **Deploy cloud services**. When you click that option, you get many more deployment choices, from a single virtual server to a service using stacks, as Figure 8.4 shows.

Figure 8.4: Cloud-services deployment options

Choose **Deploy a cloud service using patterns**. This provisioning option uses a virtual system pattern. Figure 8.5 shows the list of available patterns, some of which will look familiar from our discussion of virtual system patterns in the context of

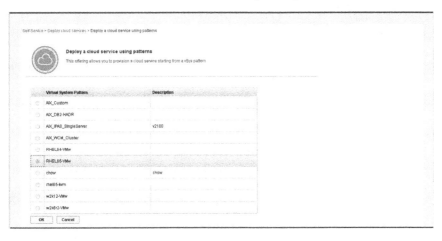

Figure 8.5: Choosing a pattern to deploy

the IBM PureApplication System in Chapter 3. Choose a VMware-based image; our example uses one named RHEL65-VM.

After selecting the pattern from the list, click **OK**. The Virtual System Instance Details screen shown in Figure 8.6 will appear and give you the option to change the instance name. Make sure you choose the environment profile, and then schedule the deployment. This screen should look familiar; it's similar to what we saw when deploying a virtual system pattern on the PureApplication System.

Figure 8.6: Instance details about the pattern to be deployed

When you click **OK**, the subsequent screen will show more details about the parts of the pattern and script packages, if any. You'll need to click **OK** once again to submit the deployment request. You can then select the **REQUEST HISTORY** menu option and watch the status of the deployment.

ICO and the PureApplication System

We've seen how a cloud service can be deployed in ICO using a virtual system pattern. That capability exists because a version of the pattern engine from Pure-Application is embedded in ICO.

One of the options in the ICO console menu is named **PATTERNS.** When you click it, you get a sub-menu that lists Instances, Pattern Design, Deployer Configuration, and Deployer Administration. The selections under each of those choices are the same ones we saw in the PureApplication workload and system consoles. Table 8.3 lists the PATTERNS sub-menu choices.

Table 8.3: Pattern sub-menus and choices in ICO

PATTERNS Sub-menu	Choices
Instances	Virtual System Instances
	Virtual System Instances (Classic)
	Virtual Application Instances
	Shared Services Instances
Pattern Design	Virtual System Patterns
	Virtual System Patterns (Classic)
	Virtual Application Patterns
	Virtual System Templates
	Virtual Application Templates
	Virtual Images
	DB2 Images (Virtual Systems)
	Script Packages
	Add-Ons
	Orchestration Actions

Continued

PATTERNS Sub-menu	Choices	*Continued*
Deployer Configuration	IP Groups	
	Cloud Groups	
	Environment Profiles	
	Shared Services	
	System Plug-ins	
	Pattern Types	
	Default Deploy Settings	
	Components Definition	
	IBM Installation Manager Repository	
	Emergency Fixes	
	DB2 Fix Packs (Virtual Systems)	
Deployer Administration	Settings	
	Troubleshooting	

Metering and Chargeback in ICO Enterprise Edition

Recall that we discussed monitoring and chargeback in Chapter 5. ICO Enterprise Edition has a monitoring and cost management feature that produces cloud services usage data per VM. This data can be integrated with other software to produce metering data and chargeback reports.

ICO Enterprise Edition collects data such as information about architecture, the number of virtual CPUs allocated, allocated memory (GB), allocated disk (TB), the operating system deployed, and the deployed image. The metering data is collected at the OpenStack level, and ICO provides rate templates or tables for infrastructure charges. These rates provide a chargeback mechanism for how long cloud resources have been reserved, but not necessarily in use.

Overview of OpenStack

We've mentioned OpenStack quite a bit, so let's take a look at it. OpenStack (*www .openstack.org)* is open-source software that allows deployment and management of cloud infrastructure as a service (IaaS). It supports both private and public cloud deployments and fulfills two requisites of cloud services: scalability and simplicity.

Written in Python, the OpenStack software is highly configurable and can be used to control large pools of compute, storage, and networking resources throughout a datacenter. Resources can be managed through a dashboard (*www.openstack.org/ software/openstack-dashboard*) or via the OpenStack APIs (*developer.openstack.org*). You can choose from different hypervisors that it supports, such as Xen, VMware, and KVM. OpenStack also supports bare-metal configuration.

Several shared services span the three pillars of compute, storage, and networking required for implementing and operating clouds. Table 8.4 lists the various OpenStack services and the code names by which they're commonly known.

Table 8.4: OpenStack services

Code name	Service	Role
Nova	Compute	OpenStack Nova provides an API to dynamically request and configure virtual servers. Nova is a cloud computing fabric controller, which is the main part of an IaaS system. It is designed to manage and automate pools of computer resources.
Cinder	Block Storage	Cinder provides persistent block-level storage devices for use with OpenStack compute instances. It manages the creation, attachment, and detachment of the block devices to servers.
Swift	Object Storage	Swift is a scalable redundant storage system. Objects and files are written to multiple disk drives spread throughout servers, and the OpenStack software is responsible for ensuring data replication and integrity across the cluster.
Neutron	Network	Neutron is a scalable virtual networking service. Technology-agnostic, it allows VM interfaces (vNICs) to connect to other OpenStack services such as Nova.
Keystone	Authentication	Keystone provides identity, token, catalog, and policy services. It manages user databases and OpenStack service catalogs and their API endpoints. Keystone integrates with existing back-end directory services such as LDAP.
Heat	Orchestration Service	Heat uses HOT templates to launch and manage composite cloud applications. It describes infrastructure resources and their relationships.
Ceilometer	Billing Service	Ceilometer measures utilization of the physical and virtual resources utilized in deployed clouds. The data is saved for subsequent retrieval and analysis.
Glance	Image Service	Glance provides discovery, registration, and delivery services for disk and server images. Stored images can be used as templates to get new servers up and running quickly and more consistently.

Continued

Code name	Service	Role	*Continued*
Horizon	Dashboard	Horizon is a Web-based user interface to OpenStack services including Nova, Swift, and Keystone. It lets you configure, deploy, and manage the services.	
Trove	Database Service	Trove is a database-as-a-service (DBaaS) provisioning relational and non-relational database engine that runs entirely on OpenStack.	

Overview of Chef

Chef is mainly used as an IT infrastructure automation tool that lets you describe how your machines should be set up. In other words with Chef, you can automate how you build, deploy, and manage your systems and Cloud infrastructure. Chef is written primarily in Ruby and uses *cookbooks* and *recipes* to provision and configure new physical and virtual machines upon which applications can be deployed. The related command-line tool is called *knife*.

Cookbooks and recipes are abstract definitions describing how a specific part of the infrastructure should be built and managed. When those definitions are applied to servers and applications, the result is an automated infrastructure. The cookbooks and recipes assist in creating identical infrastructures. When a new node is activated or added, the Chef client needs to know which cookbook or recipe to apply.

Note: Recipes are what you write to install and configure software components on the hardware. A cookbook is a collection of one or more related recipes. For example, the WebSphere Application Server v8.5 cookbook includes two recipes: was85::dmgr and was85::node.

Because Chef uses Ruby, in the user interface you will see filenames with the .rb extension. Ruby is a simple programming language used to define the patterns that are found in resources, recipes, and cookbooks. Figure 8.7 shows the folder structure. The folder named recipes contains all the Chef recipe files.

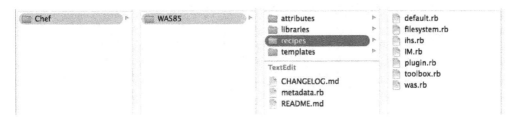

Figure 8.7: Chef's recipe folder structure

Too help with this quick overview of Chef, let's look at a sample recipe. Listing 8.1 shows an actual Chef recipe for installing WebSphere Application Server V8.5. You can see that the file looks a lot like a script file, in that it invokes the appropriate commands to install, configure, and start the resources.

```
##Install WebSphere Application Server 8.5

execute "WebSphere install" do

  command "/apps/WebSphere/InstallationManager/eclipse/tools/imcl
-acceptLicense -input /mnt/software/WAS85/responsefiles/
responsefile_was.nd.xml -showProgress"

  action :run

  creates "/apps/WebSphere/AppServer-8.5"

end


##Create Cell Profile

execute "Dmgr Profile" do
```
Continued

Listing 8.1: Chef recipe for installing and starting WebSphere Application Server

Continued

```
  command "/apps/WebSphere/AppServer-8.5/bin/manageprofiles.sh -create
-profileName myProfile -profilepath /apps/WebSphere/AppServer-8.5/profiles/
myProfile -templatepath /apps/WebSphere/AppServer-8.5/profileTemplates/cell/
dmgr -serverType DEPLOYMENT_MANAGER -cellName Cell01 -hostName localhost
-nodeName node01 -startingPort 9900 -isDefault -enableAdminSecurity true
-adminUserName wasadmin -adminPassword wasadmin -nodeProfilePath /apps/
WebSphere/AppServer-8.5/profiles/AppSrv01 -appServerNodeName node01"

  action :run

  creates "/apps/WebSphere/AppServer-8.5/profiles/myProfile"

end


execute "App Server Profile" do

  command "/apps/WebSphere/AppServer-8.5/bin/manageprofiles.sh -create
-profileName node01 -profilepath /apps/WebSphere/AppServer-8.5/profiles/node01
-templatepath /apps/WebSphere/AppServer-8.5/profileTemplates/cell/default
-dmgrProfilePath /apps/WebSphere/AppServer-8.5/profiles/myProfile -portsFile /
apps/WebSphere/AppServer-8.5/profiles/myProfile/properties/nodeportdef.props
-cellName Cell01 -nodeName myProfile_node01 -appServerNodeName node01"

  action :run

  creates "/apps/WebSphere/AppServer-8.5/profiles/node01"

end


##Start the Dmgr

execute "Start Dmgr" do

  command "su wasadm -c '/apps/WebSphere/AppServer-8.5/profiles/myProfile/bin/
startManager.sh -username wasadm -password password'"

  action :run

end
```

Continued

```
                                                          Continued
##Synch AppServer node

execute "Synch Node" do

  command "su wasadm -c '/apps/WebSphere/AppServer-8.5/profiles/AppSrv01/bin/
syncNode.sh localhost 9903 -username wasadm -password password'"

  action :run

end


##Start WebSphere AppServer Node

execute "Start AppServer" do

  command "su wasadm -c '/apps/WebSphere/AppServer-8.5/profiles/AppSrv01/bin/
startNode.sh'"

  action :run

end
```

Before you actually start cooking, you'll want to learn more about Chef. One of the best resources is the Chef documents available at *docs.chef.io/chef_overview.html*.

Cloudlets

As cloud deployments increase, especially those involving heterogeneous platforms, cloud orchestration is becoming a necessity. Products such as IBM Cloud Orchestrator allow enterprises to deliver process orchestration, workload orchestration, and resource orchestration. Components from OpenStack provide much needed interoperability between systems. Monitoring and chargeback, discussed in Chapter 5, is another important service provided by orchestration tools. Salt, a new, Python-based open-source configuration management tool, can also be used for configuring and managing cloud infrastructure. You can download the software at https://pypi .python.org/pypi/salt.

Reference

- IBM Cloud Orchestrator components: *www-01.ibm.com/support/knowledge center/SS4KMC_2.4.0/com.ibm.sco.doc_2.4/c_cloud_orchestrator_ components.html*

9

Hybrid Cloud

In Chapter 3, we talked about patterns of expertise—encapsulations of installation and configuration best practices available on IBM's PureApplication System. Patterns of expertise have been so well received that customers have requested they be made available in the public cloud. Those types of patterns could be valuable if the pattern engine could operate in the public cloud. Chapter 5 discussed public cloud platforms, including IBM's SoftLayer. After listening to its customers, IBM took the next step and ported the pattern engine to SoftLayer, allowing users to run those software patterns, as a service, in the public cloud.

We have covered the salient features of PureApplication System and SoftLayer and have seen patterns in action in the preceding chapters. In this chapter we shall see how they all come together by describing the steps to deploy another popular middleware pattern, namely IBM Integration Bus, or IIB, on SoftLayer. IIB (formerly known as WebSphere Message Broker) is IBM's integration broker from the WebSphere product family.

The creation of on-premises PaaS development platforms, which IBM has implemented in Bluemix Dedicated, is a revealing example of what can happen when an IT company listens to a rapidly changing market and ensures that its products evolve to meet that market's needs. Chapter 6 touched upon what Bluemix Dedicated is and how it can become part of a hybrid cloud solution.

Hybrid Cloud Overview

A hybrid is a mixture or fusion of two different elements. Hybrid cars, for example, are a combination of a gasoline engine and an electric motor, with both having the ability to propel the vehicle. A hybrid cloud combines the resources available in a private cloud with those in the public cloud while both continue to function as independent and unique entities. Thus, a hybrid cloud offers the benefits of multiple deployment models. Why not use just a public cloud or a private cloud? The answer lies in economics, speed, and privacy, which are the major forces that drive enterprises to hybrid cloud solutions.

 Note: A private cloud that uses public cloud services and has one or more touch points to the public cloud is the genesis of a hybrid cloud solution.

A better definition would be to use the terms *on-premises* and *off-premises* to describe the location of the services. A hybrid solution is created when private (on-premises) and public (off-premises) services are used together. For example, a company using a Software as a Service (SaaS) application that accesses the private data in the company's data center is using a hybrid cloud solution. Another example is using a public cloud development platform such as IBM Bluemix to create an app that also accesses private data from an on-premises database. Some data can be public and stored in the public cloud, but other data, for compliance and privacy reasons, has to be secured, which means it resides in a private store or on-premises.

The public cloud and private cloud communicate with each other over a secure encrypted connection. Thus, companies can store private data in a private cloud and use it in an app that leverages computational resources from a public cloud. Figure 9.1 shows the classic depiction of a hybrid cloud. The Layer 2 connection means that on either end of the connection the same subnet/VLAN exists and is used as the data link.

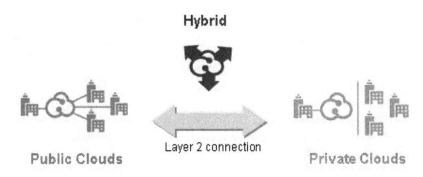

Figure 9.1: Hybrid cloud depiction

Note: The seven layers of the Open Systems Interconnection (OSI) model are:

- Layer 7: application layer
- Layer 6: presentation layer
- Layer 5: session layer
- Layer 4: transport layer
- Layer 3: network layer
- Layer 2: data link layer
- Layer 1: physical layer

Scaling the cloud delivery model to an Internet scale is best achieved by improvements in the layers 4-7 infrastructure.

Hybrid cloud models are offered by several different types of cloud providers. A private cloud provider may offer a hybrid cloud by teaming up with a public cloud provider. A case in point is Apprenda®, which teams up with Microsoft Azure. A single cloud provider may offer both public and private clouds, as does IBM. Or organizations that manage their own private cloud may sign up for a public cloud service, which they then integrate into their infrastructure, resulting in a hybrid cloud.

Note: Information is never an all-or-nothing scenario. You keep some information within your private domain, and the rest is open to the public. That is as true in cloud computing as it is in life.

Hybrid Cloud Topologies

Because the public IBM Bluemix platform and IBM Bluemix Dedicated runtimes and services are hosted on the same data center and operate in the same SoftLayer infrastructure, the combined solution of public and dedicated Bluemix doesn't fall into the category of a hybrid cloud solution. A hybrid solution must have an on-premises component that exchanges data with an off-premises resource.

Figure 9.2 depicts several topologies that use some of the products mentioned in this book and do qualify as hybrid clouds, such as PureApplication System making use of services running in Bluemix, public Bluemix using data from a database server in the data center, and an application running in the SoftLayer public cloud while accessing a secure back-end system on-premises. One example in Figure 9.2 depicts PureApplication Service on SoftLayer interacting with PureApplication System. The next section talks about PureApplication Service.

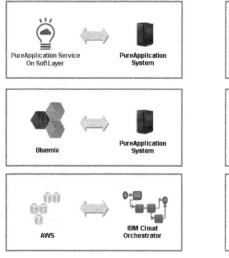
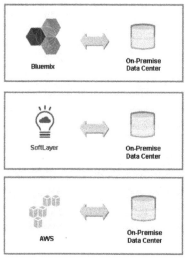

Figure 9.2: Sample hybrid cloud topologies

Hybrid cloud solutions provide many advantages for enterprises, but there are certain scenarios in which they don't work. For example, a hybrid cloud solution is not a good idea for mission-critical operations or when enterprises are afraid to send sensitive data over a public network. But the pros usually seem to outweigh the cons, hence the explosion of vendors offering hybrid cloud solutions. From a cost perspective, hybrid clouds are more expensive than public clouds but less costly than private clouds. Probably the best scenario is to have a private cloud that runs normal workloads and has bursting capability to the public cloud when there is scale-up demand.

PureApplication Service on SoftLayer

IBM PureApplication System provides a way to virtualize, dispense, optimize, and monitor software applications in the cloud. Preconfigured and preoptimized topologies that are packaged as patterns in a hypervisor image lie at the core of this expert integrated system or converged system.

 Note: A pattern in this context is a logical description of both physical and virtual assets that together provide a particular solution.

Figure 9.3 shows the three form factors of PureApplication: System, Service, and Software. PureApplication Software can be installed on any hardware running VMware.

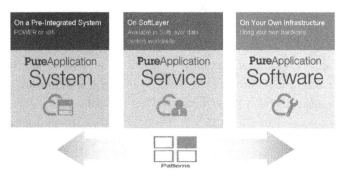

Figure 9.3: PureApplication form factors

The PureApplication Service is built with dedicated SoftLayer hardware, which includes its own compute, network, and storage components to achieve complete application isolation. The workload interface is identical to that of PureApplication System, which allows for portability of software patterns across on-premises and off-premises clouds without the need to redesign solutions.

PureApplication Service consists of three main components:

- PureApplication Service infrastructure, which includes dedicated bare-metal servers of from 4 to 16 cores

- PureApplication Service platform, which includes PureApplication monitoring and management with the pattern engine

- Pattern workloads, which are individual software patterns for specific workloads

Before you can use PureApplication Service, the required software must have been uploaded to the SoftLayer catalog. Additionally, the system administrator, or whoever has the necessary authority, must on-board you and provide the login credentials you need to access the system. *On-boarding* a user means establishing a user account that is totally isolated from other users, populating the user account with one or more dedicated and isolated instances and with storage, and deploying required patterns from the catalog into the user's environment.

 Note: Each SoftLayer Server instance comes with 1 TB of storage, with the option to add more in increments of 1 TB.

Figure 9.4 shows three user accounts created with varying server instances and storage. Client1 and Client3 are close to SoftLayer Site A and thus are tethered to Datacenter A, while Client2 is provisioned at Datacenter B.

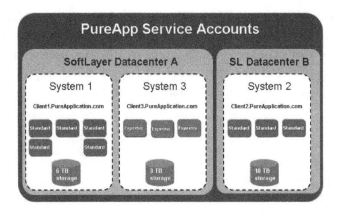

Figure 9.4: PureApplication Service accounts

PureApplication infrastructure on SoftLayer is available in three configurations, known as eSeries, mSeries, and sSeries. Figure 9.5 shows the details for those configurations. Because of the dynamic nature of the cloud, it is always recommended that you double-check the available configurations with your SoftLayer administrator.

	eSeries (e24)	mSeries (m128)	sSeries (s256)
Processor	Single Processor Quad Core Xeon 3450	Single Processor Octo Core Xeon 2670	Double Processor Octo Core Xeon 2670
Processor Speed	2.66 GHz	2.60 GHz	2.60 GHz
Processor Cache	8 MB	20 MB	20 MB
Cores	4 cores	8 cores	16 cores
PVUs	280 PVUs (4 x 70 PVU)	560 PVUs (8 x 70 PVU)	1,120 PVUs (16 x 70 PVU)
Memory Type	DDR3 Registered 1333	DDR3 Registered 1333	DDR3 Registered 1333
Memory Amount	24 GB	128 GB	256 GB
Public Bandwidth	Unlimited Bandwidth	Unlimited Bandwidth	Unlimited Bandwidth
Uplink Port Speed	1 Gbps Private 1 Gbps Public	2 Gbps Private 2 Gbps Public	2 Gbps Private 2 Gbps Public
Storage Type	HDD SAN (iSCSI)	HDD SAN (iSCSI)	HDD SAN (iSCSI)
Storage Amount	1 TB	1 TB	1 TB
Storage Redundancy	RAID 50	RAID 50	RAID 50

Figure 9.5: PureApplication configurations on SoftLayer

From an architecture perspective, let's take a look at how things are set up with PureApplication Service on SoftLayer. As Figure 9.6 illustrates, one or more virtualized environments are configured and managed by IBM. On each environment, the client can deploy patterns using a certain cloud group and IP group. After a successful deployment, the client can install and manage the workloads.

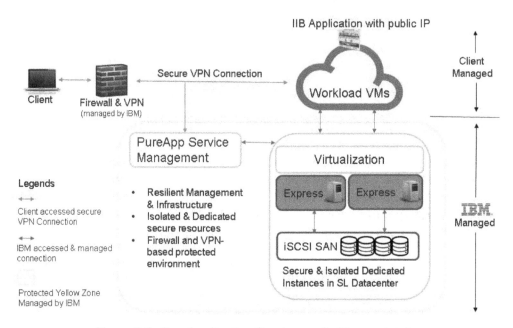

Figure 9.6: PureApplication Service on SoftLayer details

 Note: The cloud shape in Figure 9.6 indicates the IBM intranet, and the large rectangular outlined area is the IBM extranet.

Once a customer understands the infrastructure details, the next question that normally arises is what software, if any, are PureApplication Service users entitled to? Table 9.1 lists all the entitled and preloaded software products and services that are included in the price of PureApplication Service. Details and white papers are available at *www.ibm.com/ibm/puresystems/us/en/hybrid-cloud*.

Table 9.1: Software included with PureApplication Service on SoftLayer

Pattern	Pre-entitled	Preloaded
Caching Service	Y	Y
Proxy Service	Y	Y
ITM Monitoring Service	Y	Y
IBM Image Construction & Composition Tool Pattern	Y	Y
Red Hat Base OS Image	Y	Y
IBM Application Pattern for Java	Y	Y

As explained in Chapter 3, three types of patterns are available on Pure-Application V2: virtual system patterns, virtual application patterns, and virtual system classic patterns.

- Virtual system patterns provide the most flexibility and customization options of the two types of virtual system patterns. You can choose an operating system to run the pattern on, and then you can add scaling policies to the pattern.

- Virtual application patterns are highly optimized and are constructed solely for the purpose of supporting a single workload. The integrated software includes only the features and functions that are required. This pattern requires the least amount of customization during deployment and provides the fastest return on investment.

- Virtual system classic patterns provide all flexibility and customization options. A classic pattern consists of an operating system and, potentially, additional IBM software solutions, such as WebSphere Application Server or IBM Business Process Management.

 Note: A SoftLayer instance that is running PureApplication System V1 includes only the virtual system classic pattern and virtual application pattern.

For more information about patterns, see *www.ibm.com/developerworks/cloud/library/cl-puresystem-vsp/index.html*.

Working with PureApplication Service on SoftLayer

Other than the marquee on the login page, the user interface to PureApplication Service on SoftLayer, also known as PureSystem Manager, looks very much like the IBM PureApplication System interface. PureApplication Service on SoftLayer has a single console, shown in Figure 9.7, that's akin to the PureApplication System workload console. You'll notice that there is no System sub-menu because all the system-related tasks are handled by the IBM, which hosts the cloud.

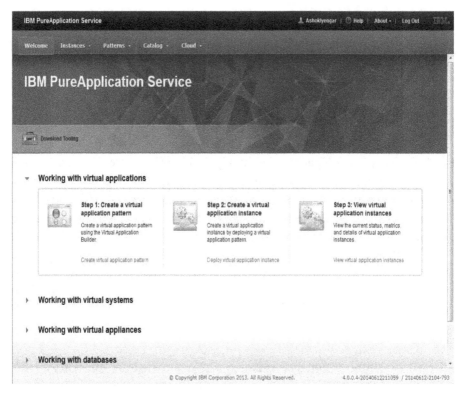

Figure 9.7: PureApplication Service console

To check the catalog and view available hypervisor images, select **Catalog >
Virtual Images**. If you don't find the image you want, you'll need to contact the
SoftLayer support team.

 Tip: All system-related tasks are managed by the IBM cloud
hosting team—in the case of PureApplication Service on
SoftLayer, that's the SoftLayer hosting team.

Like the PureApplication System, the PureApplication Service console's
Welcome tab has a Download Tooling link. Figure 9.8 shows the tooling options.

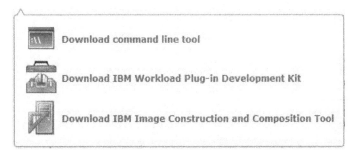

Figure 9.8: Tooling options in PureApplication Service console

After downloading the command-line tool, unzip the executable to a folder,
preferably C:\IBM\Deployer. Then you can use the command-line interface tool
from a pattern perspective, just as you do on PureApplication System.

Working with the IIB Pattern

In Chapter 3, we went through the process of deploying the IBM Business Process
Manager pattern using a virtual system classic pattern because that's what we uploaded in PureApplication System. Here we'll use a virtual system classic pattern to give
you a taste of the IIB. There was no special reason for choosing the IIB pattern other
than as an example.

First, the IIB hypervisor image must be available. Assuming it is, go to **Catalog > Virtual Images** and highlight **IBM Integration Bus 9.0.0.0**. You'll see the details in the main pane (Figure 9.9). In addition to the version and image reference number, notice that there are two versions of the IIB pattern: IBM Integration Bus 9.0.0.0 Basic and IBM Integration Bus 9.0.0.0 Advanced. Clicking either of those links will take you to the patterns page.

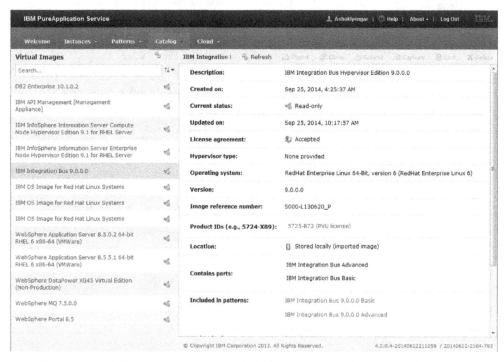

Figure 9.9: IIB Patterns available with PureApplication Service on SoftLayer

Click the IIB Basic pattern link. You will be taken to the Virtual System Patterns screen, which is under the Patterns sub-menu. Figure 9.10 shows the screen; note that the pattern is rather simple, with only one virtual machine (VM) denoted in the pink box at the bottom of the canvas. Other details of the pattern are also displayed. You'll observe that the value of the **In the cloud now** field is **none**, because we haven't yet deployed the pattern.

176

Figure 9.10: IIB Basic Pattern details

 Tip: Always make a clone of a pattern before modifying it.

You can deploy the pattern by clicking the **Deploy** link at the top. Most patterns have parameters associated with them, and the IIB pattern is no exception. As you'd expect, the advanced version of the pattern has a lot more parameters than does the basic version.

The IIB pattern contains just one virtual part. You'll have to provide a unique virtual system name, choose the environment or cloud group, and then configure the IBM Integration Bus part.

Choose a name that helps you identify the instance and the environment. When choosing the environment, you can also select the IP version and the cloud group. In the case of PureApplication Service, the SoftLayer administrator will let you know which cloud group and IP group to use. The deployment will be scheduled immediately unless you choose to schedule it for a later day or time.

You'll also need to choose the number of virtual CPUs and the memory size. For starters, you can use the defaults of one CPU and 2048 MB of memory. If necessary, you can increase those values later. Finally, you'll enter the passwords for the two default users, root and virtuser, as in Figure 9.11. When you're finished, click **OK**.

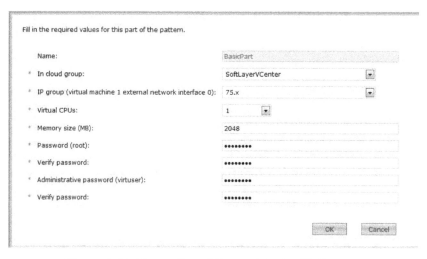

Figure 9.11: Properties of the part in the IIB Pattern

When all required configuration parameters are filled in, you'll see check marks by each field on the deployment summary screen, as in Figure 9.12. You can then click **OK** to schedule deployment of the IIB pattern. After the instance is deployed, you can highlight it to see the details.

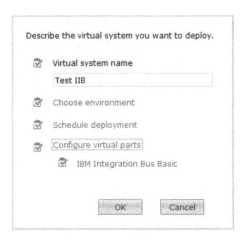

Figure 9.12: Properties of the part in the IIB Pattern

With the IIB instance up and running, you can verify the installation by opening a command window in the VM and running the command dspmqver, which should display version details. Then the instance can be used as you would normally work with a running IIB instance.

Let's stop for a moment and think of what was accomplished. PureApplication Service on SoftLayer helps extend your private cloud applications to the public cloud. In other words, you can now quickly and inexpensively develop, deploy, and test applications in a public cloud and then, if need be, bring the finished product on-premises to the private cloud without having to redesign the app or its underlying infrastructure.

To complete the hybrid cloud story, you can set up a "local" IIB pattern instance running on PureApplication System, which would be an on-premises cloud. Alternatively, you can configure message queues on traditional servers and send messages to the remote queues; that approach would require setting up a secure pipe between the on-premises environment and the off-premises environment. Let's look at how that's done.

IPSec VPN Setup

The most important part of setting up a hybrid cloud solution is configuring a secure tunnel that gives VPN clients secure access to corporate resources via IPsec while permitting unsecured access to the Internet. You can find many articles with detailed setup instructions from networking companies such as Cisco® and Brocade Communications Systems.

It helps to have the same type of gateway on both sides. If not, the steps to set up the tunnel will be a bit different for each side depending on the type of gateway. IBM's SoftLayer uses a Brocade® Vyatta® gateway. Once a site-to-site VPN is configured, the communication channel is established between each subnet on one site and all subnets on the other site. Then a VM on Site 1—in our example, the IIB instance running in PureApplication Service on SoftLayer—will be able to communicate with a VM on Site 2, possibly an IIB instance in the PureApplication System on-premises. Figure 9.13 shows a generic site-to-site IPSec VPN configuration.

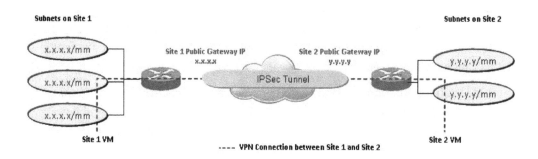

Figure 9.13: Site-to-site IPSec VPN

Tip: Only subnets that need access via a site-to-site VPN should be configured. Once that is established, firewall rules are needed on both sides to allow traffic to go back and forth.

Cloudlets

PureApplication Service on SoftLayer is a good example of extending your applications to the hybrid cloud. Businesses can then harness the power of patterns by developing on the cloud and deploying applications on-premises while allowing the use of off-premises resources when needed.

The screenshots in this chapter are from a trial version of PureApplication Service. The customer version of PureApplication Service on SoftLayer has been upgraded to V2 with the latest fix packs.

The Bluemix Dedicated platform makes the most sense as a common development platform for an enterprise with the ability to run segregated workloads. One common scenario clients are looking at is hosting the application on a public cloud while keeping the database on-premises. You can easily see how these cloud platforms can be used in different topologies to create a hybrid cloud environment.

This page intentionally left blank.

Index